SEEDS OF
REPRESSION

SEEDS OF REPRESSION

Harry S. Truman
and the
Origins of McCarthyism

by
ATHAN THEOHARIS

Quadrangle Books
CHICAGO • 1971

Library of Congress Catalog Card Number: 71–116089
SBN 8129–0169–X

For Nancy

Preface

In THE early 1950's Joseph R. McCarthy, junior Senator from Wisconsin, came to dominate American politics and to symbolize the phenomenon now called "McCarthyism." Relying on charges of "communists in government" and accusing American leaders of being "soft toward communism," Senator McCarthy and his followers attributed America's Cold War problems to subversive influence in the formulation of United States government policy. Their objective was not simply to remove that influence and alter the direction of United States policy but to discredit the administrations of Franklin D. Roosevelt and Harry S. Truman and, indirectly, the reform measures associated with the New Deal and Fair Deal. McCarthyism was not, however, an overtly conservative—that is, an anti-reformist—political movement. It drew its strength from popular concerns over national security, fears of internal subversion, and the people's underlying frustration with the costs and complexity of the Cold War.

McCarthyism offered no program to insure security. Instead, its approach, almost wholly negative, involved an emotional reaction to Cold War problems, chiefly an explanation of "conspiracy" for complex issues, that was attractive because it was simplistic. McCarthy's charges of communist influence in fact paralleled, in an exaggerated way, the popular obsession with national security that arose after World War II. The Truman administration committed itself to victory over communism and to safeguarding the nation from external and internal threats; the rhetoric of McCarthyism was in this sense well within the framework of Cold War politics. The Senator and the administration differed not so much over ends as over means and emphasis.

McCarthyism perceived subversives in Washington, not Soviet power or strategic realities, as the major obstacle to achieving "victory over communism." This focus on internal subversion distinguished the Senator and his followers from Cold Warriors within the Truman administration as well as from earlier conservative critics of the New Deal.

Since the 1930's congressional conservatives had sought to discredit FDR's policies by charging communist influence was behind them. After World War II, and especially in dramatic, well-staged, and well-publicized hearings during 1947 and 1948, the House Committee on Un-American Activities reiterated these charges. During the 1950's McCarthy and his conservative congressional supporters focused on national security rather than political reform. With the postwar confrontation between Russia and the West as a backdrop, they assailed the administration's loyalty program as well as its foreign policy. The administration's security measures, they charged, were inadequate because the administration itself was sympathetic toward communism or ignorant of its threat. Foreign policy was a failure because pro-Soviet or disloyal employees in the State Department and elsewhere had helped to formulate and execute it.

In the political climate produced by these charges, the Truman administration found it impossible to use its own anti-communist record to advantage, or to make political capital out of the fact that McCarthy's followers had often failed to support such measures as NATO, the Truman Doctrine, and universal military training. As fiscal conservatives, isolationists, and opponents of a strong executive, during the period 1945 through 1949 they had dissented from the Truman administration's attempts to contain communism. Their anti-communism relied on verbal bluff, not military power. Their earlier concern over subversion had centered not on foreign espionage or sabotage but on what they believed to be the un-Americanism of domestic dissenters. Yet Truman's efforts to discredit McCarthy and his followers proved unconvincing and, ironically, even counterproductive.

In point of fact, as I argue in the pages that follow, McCarthyism derived its effectiveness from (1) the changed political climate that came with the intensification of the Cold War, and (2) President Truman's loss of credibility. The Cold War created the context, and Truman's rhetoric and leadership the political vacuum, that made the charges and appeals of McCarthyism not merely viable but persuasive to a great many Americans. Truman's loss of credibility stemmed partly from the nature of his rhetoric and the priority of his policies, and partly from the way he responded to McCarthyite charges. His difficulties were reinforced by a series of events at home and abroad in 1949 and 1950 which, seemingly, confirmed the existence of a subversive threat.

McCarthyism, then, was no aberration. It was a political movement in touch with the major concerns of Cold War politics. Its emergence dramatized the connection between foreign policy and domestic politics—specifically, the way in which a suspicious, militaristic approach to foreign policy, emphasizing the subversive character of the Soviet threat, substantively altered the domestic political climate. The intensification of the Cold War, both because of the U.S.-Soviet conflict and Truman's rhetoric, changed national priorities and values, and in so doing created a distinctly conservative mood whose primary commitment was to absolute security and the status quo.

Acknowledgments

THE OPPORTUNITY to complete the research and writing of this study was made possible by financial grants from the Truman Institute for National and International Affairs and Wayne State University. I also acknowledge the typing assistance of Marquette University, particularly Miss Ann Koenig. My former colleagues at Wayne State, Melvin Small, Lynn Parsons, Stanley Shapiro, and Otto Feinstein, offered both stylistic and substantive criticisms, sharpening the discussion and analysis. Barton Bernstein of Stanford University and Michael Rogin of the University of California at Berkeley read the rough draft of the manuscript; their knowledge of the period helped me to reduce errors of fact and interpretation. Walter Johnson, formerly of the University of Chicago and presently on the faculty of the University of Hawaii, aroused my interest in the politics of the Cold War; my parents, brothers, and sisters enabled me to complete my formal education.

Ivan Dee, my editor at Quadrangle, offered help beyond the responsibilities of an editor. His demanding perfectionism honed my prose into more readable form, and his advice on organization and focus greatly improved the manuscript. No acknowledgment can fully describe my indebtedness to him as editor and friend.

My wife Nancy's loving support and encouragement, and her own help as editor and critic, sustained me during moments of frustration and depression. Without her love, I would not have completed this study.

For errors in fact and interpretation I alone, of course, am responsible.

Contents

SEEDS OF
REPRESSION

1

The Mood of

Popular Anti-Communism

---

*There was a time when a man might entertain a few
general political principles and apply them with some confidence. A citizen believed in states' rights or in a centralized federal government; in free trade or protection. It did
not involve much mental strain to imagine that by throwing
in his lot with one party or another he could so express his
views that his belief would count in government. For the
average voter today . . . at election time, appeals to some
time-worn slogan may galvanize him into a temporary
notion that he has conviction on an important subject, but
. . . [his] belief lacks the qualities which attach to belief
about matters of personal concern.*
                              —JOHN DEWEY, *The Public and Its Problems*

THOUGH IN THE above quotation Dewey was talking about
the tariff issue in particular, he touches on some of the
problems unique to twentieth-century American politics. The
public is not uninterested in major national issues; its apparent apathy or lack of conviction at times has been the
product both of the complexity of these issues and the un-
responsive character of the major parties and decision-making

3

institutions. Formally, American political institutions may have appeared democratic; operationally, they serve to minimize the public's role and influence.

As the United States expanded territorially, as its economy diversified and its corporations became dominant, and as its socio-economic problems became national in scope, the individual citizen faced new questions of a complexity beyond his immediate understanding or personal experience. At the same time, traditional political institutions that had formerly offered one means to exert popular influence on the legislative process were radically altered. In the late nineteenth and early twentieth centuries, highly professional and efficient party organizations and the institutional structure of Congress, based on the committee system and seniority, succeeded in imposing limits to political debate or otherwise defusing popular pressure. Popular influence on the legislative process or the determination of priorities was effectively reduced; public opinion became less important; disaffection could be undercut by the enactment of seeming reform measures or by emotional appeals to traditional values and symbols.

As one result of these developments, a feeling of exclusion and impotence on the part of the body politic became evident. This, in turn, contributed to a vacillating popular response of passivity or protest, in which the electorate at times uncritically followed the lead of incumbent leaders and parties, while at other times, especially during periods of crisis, it responded to the charges of the party out of power.

Throughout the twentieth century, most Americans have never completely accepted this form of exclusionary, structured politics as a fact of our political life. The democratic rhetoric of political debate and the democratic character of the political party system, moreover, have sustained a popular belief in the responsiveness of our political institutions. Thus many Americans, when confronted by unexpected, disruptive crises, respond politically with a negative, often embittered emotionalism, their protest only endorsing the need for a greater popular voice in government. This situation has made it possible for the "outs" to engage in irresponsible tactics: they can assail the men and policies of the incumbent party and call for "reform" without clearly delineating alternative policies that will either resolve the problems that brought about the crisis or democratize the political system.

Excluding the public from substantively influencing basic political decisions has created a fragile system characterized by sharp changes in voter preference. The elitism of political leadership, despite its democratic rhetoric and its short-sighted commitment to the status quo, has insured a party's continuity in power only when it averts major crises and when the administration roughly upholds its rhetorical promises. This system, moreover, tends to centralize responsibility in the executive branch, with the President and his administration held responsible for major crises. Accordingly, when events dramatize contradictions between administration rhetoric and reality, popular protest appears and creates a situation that can be effectively manipulated by the "outs" —as in the Republicans' exploitation during the 1920's of Wilsonian leadership and diplomacy, the Democrats' use during the 1930's of the Republicans' seeming responsibility for the Great Depression, and Republican contentions during the 1950's that the Democrats were responsible for the communist threat to national security.

§❧

HISTORICALLY, Americans have been distinctly conservative, often responding uncritically to appeals against radicalism. This conservatism has made possible the resort to conspiratorial charges during times of national crisis which permits the attribution of problems to the influence of subversive aliens. Thus conservative politicians have often been able to propound a simple causal explanation (the existence of a conspiracy) and a ready solution (suppression or purging) for complex national problems.

Until the 1920's, however, popular anti-radicalism had not been essentially anti-communist in character. Its basic fear of domestic revolution or disorder was based on the supposed alien-subversive character of immigrants who were influenced by European anarchistic or socialistic ideas. The major groups singled out as threatening national security were the Populists, the IWW (Industrial Workers of the World), labor unions, or the Socialists. The Bolshevik Revolution of 1917, proclaiming the inevitability of international revolution, shifted attention from an internally to an externally based problem. From the Bolshevik Revolution on, radicals were seen as foreign agents or as those who sought to further the interests of a foreign power and ideology.

In part, this new view of subversion provided the basis for the Red Scare of 1919–1920. Promoted by federal officials and the business community during World War I in their combined efforts to curb the IWW and develop national unity, the Red Scare was not the product of a widely popular anti-communism, nor of an intense fear of the communist threat *per se*. Rather, the Red Scare was a conservative and nativist reaction to the disruptive political and economic changes that had altered American society since the late nineteenth century, which had been further fortified by the fears created by the United States involvement in World War I. The reaction in 1919–1920 was the product both of a popular uneasiness lest wartime prosperity be threatened by radicals and, another factor brought about by the war, a heightened intolerance toward aliens and dissenters. But since the fear of communism was not a fundamental part of this postwar conservative reaction, the Red Scare was only of temporary duration, confined to the immediate postwar years. The more pervasive aspects of anti-radicalism in these years—its true conservative and nativistic base—was revealed in the enactment of the National Origins Act regulating immigration, the acceptance of the American Plan in regard to unions, and the rise of the Ku Klux Klan.

The abrupt shift in the popular mood toward radicalism during the 1930's further reveals the pragmatic character of popular anti-communism. Overwhelmed by the devastating impact of the Great Depression, many Americans were less responsive to simple explanations of radical conspiracies, while many others turned to radicalism to resolve the economic crisis. This, combined with conservative efforts to "red bait" New Deal reforms and personnel, contributed in turn to a more sympathetic popular attitude toward communism. President Roosevelt's decision to recognize the Soviet Union in 1933 and increased concern after 1935 over the threat of fascism also helped to undercut the intensity of popular anti-communism.

Roosevelt's reformism, the threat of fascism, and the impact of the depression did not, however, altogether eliminate popular anti-communism. Instead a more temperate anti-communism evolved, one which conservatives continuously sought to exploit—most dramatically in the investigations of the House Committee on Un-American Activities—during the latter half of the 1930's to discredit Roosevelt's domestic and international policies.

With United States involvement in World War II as an ally of the Soviet Union, and the sympathetic depiction of Soviet society by the national press, Hollywood, and the Roosevelt administration, many Americans came to view the Soviet Union as a beleaguered democratic state allied with the United States in its conflict with fascism. Wartime priorities called for a more positive view of the Soviet Union. World War

II thus further reduced—but did not totally eliminate—popular anti-communism. The Cold War would reverse this process. contributing to a popular obsession with the communist threat. This development, however, was not inevitable; it was the product of changes in popular perceptions of international developments and internal security. The new obsession with communism was the result primarily of three factors: (1) Soviet actions in Eastern Europe and the Chinese Communists' success in the Far East; (2) the description of these developments in the popular press; and (3) the Truman administration's definition of realistic policy options.

§❧

IN 1945 the American public was neither uncritically responsive to anti-communist appeals nor obsessed with the communist threat. Despite Truman's desire to act unilaterally in international affairs and to rely on superior military strength, popular demands forced him to accept a rapid demobilization of American troops. The United States was, after all, committed to the United Nations, summit diplomacy, and a broad program of economic aid and development.

In the immediate postwar years Truman sought to educate the public to accept a shift in policy which emphasized the need for internal and external safeguards against a serious communist threat. Internationally, this required reliance on attaining superior military power as opposed to negotiations at the summit or through the United Nations. Similarly, communist subversion at home became a useful issue for justifying an executive-initiated loyalty program that blurred all distinctions between subversion and political radicalism.

How effective Truman's educational program was can be seen in the changes in American attitudes toward communism in the years 1945–1950, as revealed in a number of polls published by the *Public Opinion Quarterly*. (See the

Appendix.) Admittedly, the pollsters' phrasing of questions influenced the responses they obtained—a danger inherent in all public opinion polls. But these polls nevertheless reveal a striking change in the popular mood. Indeed, a reservoir of trust in the Soviet Union and an indifference toward the whole question of internal subversion had prevailed in 1945. Only with the intensification of the Cold War would these attitudes change. Decisions by policy-makers and postwar events convinced the public that a serious internal and external threat to national security existed.

The popular response was more pragmatic than ideological. In 1945, for example, many Americans were hopeful about the possibilities of accommodation with the Soviet Union (55 per cent to 31 per cent, according to one poll) and preferred working through the United Nations to resolve differences or preserve peace (56 per cent of the populace supporting the idea of a world peace force, 31 per cent a large U.S. standing army). By 1951, however, most Americans had come to view security as attainable primarily by military methods (49 per cent believing that assigning U.S. troops overseas would prevent war, 23 per cent that it would not), and were deeply distrustful of the Soviet Union.

From 1945 until the Korean War, popular support of essentially anti-Soviet policies, such as the Truman Doctrine and NATO, was consistent with administration rhetoric that these proposals were basically economic or political measures. (In 1947, for example, a majority of Americans supported economic aid to Greece but opposed military aid.) During these years, while Truman administration policy no longer relied on negotiation with the Soviet Union at the summit *or* through the United Nations, most Americans accepted at face value the administration's characterization of its containment measures as internationalist and defensive. For these reasons, most Americans could simultaneously support containment and yet hope for accommodation while remaining committed to summit diplomacy. Even though they were skeptical that diplomatic efforts could achieve peace, as late as October 1950 the majority of Americans (52 per cent to 35 per cent) supported a meeting between Truman and Stalin.

More striking, until the Korean War public opinion polls showed popular anti-communism to be ambivalent and far less militant than it appeared to be. Even after Korea, most Americans (revealed in majority support for troop withdrawal in 1951) never really construed the Korean conflict as directly threatening national security. Most Americans simply favored a rapid termination of the conflict. Polled during February 1951 about U.S. policy after Chinese Communist intervention in Korea, 61 per cent supported and only 23 per cent opposed U.S. troop withdrawals from Korea, even though 56 per cent believed that U.S. military intervention had been right and only 36 per cent that it had been wrong. Indeed, most Americans supported more vigorous efforts by the administration to reach agreement with the Chinese and North Koreans and were willing to accept the 38th parallel as a cease-fire line.

These polls further reveal the complexity of the popular response to Soviet communism. Popular anxieties reflected a distinct security consciousness, one obsessed more with Soviet power than communist ideology. Thus the public responded differently to queries about U.S. policy toward communist attempts to secure power in 1948 by distinguishing between Italian and Soviet communism. Following the Czechoslovakian coup, a plurality (47 per cent to 37 per cent) thought that the United States should attempt to suppress communist-led revolts and prevent (54 per cent to 39 per cent) any Soviet effort to control bordering territories in Europe or Asia. But most Americans (52 per cent to 28 per cent) opposed United States military intervention to prevent the prospect of an Italian Communist electoral victory.

Throughout the postwar period, moreover, whether the earlier (1945–1948) or the later (1949–1953) phase, most Americans had grave doubts about President Truman's leadership and the effectiveness of his policies. This distrust was not based on simple anti-communism, for 1948 polls reveal a striking disparity in believing, first, that Truman was opposed to "giving in" to the communists (53 per cent to 17 per cent), and yet also believing that his administration's policies were "too soft" (73 per cent).

Many Americans remained confused about the administration's priorities and objectives, and this contributed to their often contradictory reaction to its policy decisions—demanding a firmer policy yet supporting summit diplomacy. There was little consistency in the popular reaction toward the administration's China policy, despite the acceptance after 1950 of the "lost China" charge. Throughout 1945–1950, many Americans responded indifferently to suggestions that the United States provide military aid or support to the Chiang Kai-shek regime. As late as May 1949 43 per cent opposed United States involvement in the Chinese civil war (although 22 per cent supported economic or military aid to Chiang), or even the adoption of alternative military or economic methods to stop a Chinese Communist victory. This attitude changed only after Chinese Communist intervention in the Korean War when, in June 1951, a majority of Americans (54 per cent to 32 per cent) came out in favor of military aid to the Chinese Nationalists.

As with international affairs, so during the postwar period popular attitudes on loyalty-security matters revealed a heightened anti-communism. Concerned and skeptical about the loyalty of American Communists, most Americans consistently expressed support for harsh "anti-subversive" measures. Proposals advocating restrictions on the freedoms of Communists, extending to the right to speak on radio, participate in politics, or hold civil service jobs, as well as legislation requiring the registration or outlawing of Communist party membership, received general popular support. Nonetheless, at least in early 1947, many Americans could distinguish between Communists and communist sympathizers (36 per cent supported while 41 per cent opposed legislation preventing communist sympathizers from holding public office) and believed that a federal employee accused of disloyalty should not be dismissed but be given the opportunity to establish his innocence.

This lack of tolerance for the civil liberties of Communists would increase after Truman's introduction of a federal employee loyalty program in March 1947. But when Truman openly opposed the Mundt-Nixon bill, which required the registration of all members of the American Communist party, his action significantly reduced the intensity of popular anticommunism. Thus the level of support for the Mundt-Nixon bill decreased from 77 per cent in early 1948 to 63 per cent in the summer of 1948. It seems clear that the President's actions and pronouncements influenced the public temper in this instance—and no doubt on larger matters of internal security.

2

The McCarthyites:

Their Tactics and Objectives

WHILE THE TERM "McCarthyism" derives from the name and tactics of the junior senator from Wisconsin, the phenomenon involved more than a personalist, or one-man, political movement. McCarthy had a wide following in the Congress and among the public, yet his supporters as well as those who emulated his tactics were not necessarily *followers*. McCarthy's rise depended upon, as much as it contributed to, a resurgence of conservatism in the postwar Congress. Despite his following, at no time did McCarthy develop a cohesive personal political organization. This was due partly to the Senator's limited organizational abilities, partly to the congressional conservatives' mistrust of his integrity, and partly to their having different political objectives.

While conservatives in the Congress supported McCarthy's tactics and came to his defense when he was under attack during the early 1950's, they never really considered him in any sense their political leader. If McCarthyism is viewed strictly in relation to the Senator, it therefore appears amorphous and undisciplined; its dominant characteristic is the man himself, his blustering charges and tactics. If, however, McCarthyism is studied in relation to the broader political objectives of McCarthy's congressional supporters, it becomes a logical extension of traditional, conservative congressional politics. This distinction is crucial: though McCarthy and congressional conservatives after 1950 resorted to similar tactics and to a common anti-Democratic stance, the Senator concentrated primarily on foreign policy and questions of internal security, while his conservative colleagues ultimately sought to discredit the personnel, and by extension the principles, of the New Deal. In the end, the alliance between McCarthy and his congressional supporters was one not of shared goals but of convenience.

The resort to anti-radical—and more specifically, anti-communist—themes was a basic political tactic of those conservative congressmen during the postwar years who sought to impugn the New Deal. In this special sense, these conservatives were "McCarthyites" before the Senator appeared and remained so well after his censure and death. A partial, though representative, list of these men would include the following Senators: John Bricker (Republican, Ohio), Styles Bridges (Republican, New Hampshire), Homer Capehart (Republican, Indiana), Everett Dirksen (Republican, Illinois), Homer Ferguson (Republican, Michigan), William Jenner (Republican, Indiana), William Knowland (Republican, California), George Malone (Republican, Nevada), Pat McCarran (Democrat, Nevada), Karl Mundt (Republican, South Dakota), Richard Nixon (Republican, California), Robert Taft (Republican, Ohio), Herman Welker (Republican, Idaho), and Kenneth Wherry (Republican, Nebraska). In the House of Representatives, the more outspoken McCarthyites were Carl Curtis (Republican, Nebraska), George Dondero (Republican, Michigan), Charles Halleck (Republican, Indiana), Clare Hoffman (Republican, Michigan), Walter Judd (Republican, Minnesota), Charles Kersten (Republican, Wisconsin), Clare Boothe Luce (Republican, Connecticut), Joseph Martin (Republican, Massachusetts), Noah Mason (Republican, Illinois), John Rankin (Democrat, Mississippi), Daniel Reed (Republican, New York), Robert Rich (Republican, Pennsylvania), Paul Shafer (Republican, Michigan), Lawrence Smith (Republican, Wisconsin), John Taber (Republican, New York), J. Parnell Thomas (Republican, New Jersey), Charles Vursell (Republican, Illinois), and John Wood (Democrat, Georgia).*

All these Congressmen had national political influence independent of McCarthy's. Thus, while they did not strictly need him, they were not above using him during the early 1950's, adopting his tactics to their own purpose of identifying reform with subversive proclivities, and conservatism with vigilance and patriotism. Even during the early 1950's, when McCarthy had his most dramatic impact on national politics, he had little or no role in shaping conservative strategy during congressional debates on foreign policy or internal security. His congressional supporters consistently operated independently of him—at times not even bothering to consult him on important matters. Significantly, McCarthy did not play a strong role in either of the major causes of the congressional conservatives in the early 1950's: neither in the drafting and subsequent attempt to secure passage of an anti-subversive act nor in the effort to secure the nomination of a conservative for the presidency. (The initiative for the Internal Security Act of 1950 was provided by Democratic Senator Pat McCarran, chairman of the Judiciary Committee, and the Republican congressional leadership—Robert

---

* Among the news media, the more prominent McCarthy supporters included the Hearst publications; such syndicated columnists as Westbrook Pegler, George Sokolsky, Fulton Lewis, Jr., and David Lawrence; and such magazines and newspapers as *U.S. News and World Report,* the *Saturday Evening Post,* the *Chicago Tribune,* and the *Dallas Morning News.*

Taft, Styles Bridges, Kenneth Wherry, Charles Halleck, and
Joseph Martin.) True, during the 1952 presidential campaign congressional conservatives promoted McCarthy as a
public speaker and adopted his tactics to assail the Truman
administration and its personnel. Yet as a candidate for the
Republican presidential nomination they favored Senator
Robert Taft or General Douglas MacArthur. After Taft's
defeat at the Republican National Convention, these same
conservatives would support McCarthy's re-election for the
Senate, just as they would other conservative congressional
candidates. But in doing so their objective was simply to gain
control of the 83rd Congress, or at least sustain the gains
made during the 1946 senatorial and the 1950 congressional
elections.

PERSONALLY UNATTRACTIVE, McCarthy was crass and un-
principled, an unimaginative opportunist, and a distinctly
second-rate politician. In February 1950, however, he
stumbled upon a popular cause: communism in the State Department. In fact, his impact at first derived solely from this
single issue, and not from organizational support or political
identification with congressional conservatives. His now-
famous Wheeling, West Virginia, address, in which he announced that he had evidence of 205 known communists in
the State Department, was, significantly, not delivered to a
national forum but to a local Republican women's club. Nor
in his jumbled, almost incoherent and inconsistent speech to
the Senate on February 20, 1950, when he presented his
claim to possessing evidence about there being eighty-one
known "Communists in the State Department," did he re-
ceive the support of Senators Mundt, Taft, or Wherry. These

Republicans might give him considerable leeway to attack the administration, but they did not yet identify themselves with his cause. (Indeed, appraising McCarthy's senate speech, Taft stated: "It was a perfectly reckless performance.") The character of both his Wheeling and Senate speeches catapulted McCarthy to national prominence, and only when he had achieved this prominence did these conservative Congressmen champion his subsequent charges through the years 1950–1954.

From 1950 on McCarthy had no strategy for expanding on the national security issue; he was apparently content with the publicity it produced. That publicity, however, was considerable. In contrast to the earlier (1938–1948) anti-communist tactics of the pre-McCarthy conservatives, the Senator's effectiveness resulted from his citation of specific numbers, his unflinching focus on State Department personnel, and his claims that he had the documentation to support his accusations.

McCarthy's charges of State Department disloyalty dramatically raised the issue of espionage, which in turn furthered the belief that the diplomacy of past administrations had been unduly concerned with appeasing the Soviet Union. Since McCarthy's charges were neither overtly partisan nor anti-reformist, they had a broad popular appeal. Moreover, his timing was propitious: his charges followed immediately upon guilty verdicts in the Alger Hiss and Judith Coplon cases and the disclosure, in September 1949, of a successful Soviet atomic explosion. These events lent support to rumors of the time that a Soviet espionage ring had successfully permeated Washington and might continue to do so, and that administration laxity or indifference had prevented its detection.

It was the impact made by McCarthy's tactics which led congressional conservatives to support him and indeed in some instances to emulate him. By concentrating on subversion, McCarthy offered them a new method by which they could identify reform with betrayal, and thus enhance their own reputation not only as pronounced anti-communists but as domestic conservatives.

By pointing out that radicals or reformers, because of pro-Soviet leanings or naiveté in assessing Soviet objectives, had helped shape past administration foreign policy, the McCarthyites in Congress were then able to impugn the loyalty of many government employees—thereby undermining the reputation of social and economic reform—and to raise doubts about executive loyalty procedures—thereby securing popular support for restrictions on executive authority. Although the McCarthyites formally continued to rely on the technique of "guilt-by-association," their focus substantively shifted from New Deal policies and personnel to national security matters and employees in the State Department and other sensitive federal agencies. The support of congressional conservatives for the Bricker Amendment further reflected this new approach. Roosevelt's actions at Yalta became their justification for the Amendment's proposed restrictions on executive authority for foreign policy; they next hoped to use these restrictions to block domestic reform. In this sense the McCarthyites, though they adopted McCarthy's tactics, substantially transcended the Senator's rather limited objectives.

IN THE EYES of congressional conservatives, the New Deal challenged traditional conservative beliefs in limited government by establishing the federal government as a major force in national life. The New Deal's operational premise was that the federal government had the responsibility to act when state governments or the private sector were either unable or unwilling to resolve national economic problems. Injustice and economic dislocation, New Dealers held, were not inevitable; the business community and the state governments simply lacked the expertise or commitment to deal effectively with these complex national problems.

In practice, these New Deal premises had transformed twentieth-century American politics. Through the extensive use of executive powers, Roosevelt had made the presidency a direct, almost autonomous agency for political reform. Relying on such procedures as the press conference and the fireside chat, FDR reduced traditional presidential dependence on congressional leadership and the news media. Speaking directly to the public, he justified reform, initiated debates on legislation, and, in the process of doing so, reduced congressional freedom to shape public opinion or ignore public protest. In the conservative view, Roosevelt usurped legislative authority while reducing the power of the conservative congressional leadership—and at the same time forced it to respond to proposals for reform.

In their opposition to the New Deal, conservatives during the 1930's and early 1940's had naturally attacked both its political principles and Roosevelt's transformation of the presidency. In the main, they charged that the New Deal was un-American and unconstitutional, its principles and ideals alien and subversive, and Roosevelt's tactics contrary to the limited-government and checks-and-balances provisions of the Constitution. Outside conservative circles, however, these charges carried little weight, finding popular support only from those interested in limited government (Roosevelt's Supreme Court "packing" bill) or those who were uneasy over the extent of bureaucratic change that accompanied the New Deal. As such, these popular concerns, confined to institutional developments, did not reflect the charge that the ideals or methods of the New Deal were alien or subversive. By 1938 congressional conservatives were able to check Roosevelt's efforts to extend the New Deal; but they failed in their corollary purpose of discrediting New Deal reforms and personnel.

§●

UPON Harry S. Truman's accession to the presidency, his initial vacillation, indecision, and contradictory responses created an opening for those conservative Congressmen whom I have called the pre-McCarthy McCarthyites. Capitalizing on popular frustration over a series of crippling labor strikes, the retention of wartime price controls, and the slow pace of military demobilization, conservative Republicans campaigned during the 1946 congressional elections against what they believed to be the excesses of federal authority. Their campaign slogan, "Had Enough? Vote Republican," sought to exploit popular antipathy to postwar controls and Truman's "blundering" leadership.

Despite the effectiveness of this campaign tactic, it did not fully represent the broader political purposes of these conservatives. Their long-term objective, as represented in the hearings, legislative recommendations, and leadership tactics of the 80th Congress, was not only to terminate wartime controls and impose restraints on the labor unions but, more basically, to return American political life to the pre–New Deal status quo.

In 1947–1948 these Congressmen relied on two basic tactics: reducing appropriations or proposing revisionist legislation, and initiating congressional investigations of New Deal personnel. The investigations were most dramatically characterized by the hearings of the House Committee on Un-American Activities (HUAC). In its investigations of Hollywood, of federal agencies, and of the Roosevelt administration generally, the Committee sought to discredit the ideals and principles of the New Deal by disclosing possible communist influence on New Deal policies. Thus, despite their expressed concern over "espionage," these hearings really concentrated on exposing the alleged transformation of American society through "alien" legislation and ideals. Consistent with this aim, in August 1948 Whittaker Chambers accused Alger Hiss only of being a Communist party functionary. Hiss's party role, Chambers charged, had been not espionage but the promotion of communist infiltration of the New Deal.

HUAC developed these charges as background for the Republican presidential campaign of 1948, and in August of that year released an interim report summarizing its investigative purpose and findings. Its report emphasized Communist infiltration of New Deal agencies on the domestic front, but not foreign espionage nor influence on administration policy toward the Soviet Union. Domestically, the Committee stated, communists had sought to subvert and weaken American social, political, and economic institutions, thereby making the communization of America possible. Attempting to develop the espionage theme, the Committee in September 1948 belatedly contended that a wartime communist spy ring had tried to steal U.S. atomic bomb secrets. Based as it was on hearsay testimony, and without any solid documentation, this report proved to be unconvincing.

THE DEMOCRATIC VICTORY in the 1948 presidential election confronted the Republican party—and more specifically, its congressional conservatives—with an unsettling dilemma. Truman had concentrated during the campaign on the record of the New Deal and the 80th Congress. Raising the bogey of Republican responsibility for the Great Depression and linking the policies of the 80th Congress with the Republicanism of the 1920's, Truman had stirred up and made election capital of popular fears of another depression. He had also openly assailed HUAC, charging that its investigations were primarily a partisan, publicity-seeking attempt to divert public attention from the 80th Congress' "reactionary" record.

This confrontation between Truman and the Committee during the 1948 election campaign had been sharpened as the result of Truman's issuing, on March 14, an Executive Order (one, incidentally, initiated in response to a request by HUAC) generally restricting congressional access to the loyalty files of federal personnel. After the election, Truman continued his attacks on HUAC 'and its methods. In his post-election press conferences, he pointedly described his election as a popular mandate to repudiate this "defunct" committee. Concurrently, he directed Attorney General Tom Clark to draft a memorandum for use by the Democratic congressional leadership during the opening session of the 81st Congress, which outlined arguments and strategy for revising the rules of the House for the purpose of terminating the Committee.

Of even greater concern to congressional conservatives, the 1948 election results dramatized the New Deal's continuing popularity. Truman's victory could not be attributed (as Roosevelt's had been) to personal charisma or popularity. During his first three presidential years, Truman's leadership had not been strong enough to win public confidence in his abilities. Moreover, in 1948 the Democratic party was deeply divided, its popular base reduced by defections to the Dixiecrats and Progressives. Yet Truman won despite these handicaps. His success, it would seem, was made possible by the public's rejection of the overtly partisan, anti–New Deal tactics of the conservative leadership of the 80th Congress. Truman's election thus raised the question of whether the Republican party could ever win the presidency by concentrating on domestic issues and personnel.

The answer—and the Republicans' chance—came in December 1948. Whittaker Chambers' presentation of the "Pumpkin Papers"—which constituted a reversal of his earlier accusations about Hiss's functions as a Communist—not only subverted Truman's post-election strategy of terminating HUAC but provided congressional conservatives with a new issue and a new tactical approach. Chambers claimed to have received from Hiss in the 1930's microfilm of classified State Department documents, which he had hidden in a hollowed-out pumpkin on his Maryland farm. The Pumpkin Papers posed the question not of New Deal principles or the associations and beliefs of New Deal personnel, but of blatant sabotage and espionage. By shifting their focus from domestic reform to internal security, congressional conservatives were on to a tack that could have significant impact on the public. At issue was not whether the New Deal–Fair Deal administrations had transformed and weakened the American economy, but whether communist agents, by infiltrating sensitive federal agencies and betraying national secrets, had been able to promote the strategic interests of the Soviet Union within America itself. The problem for these congressional conservatives was now to convince the public that the Hiss case, far from being atypical, was representative.

Thus redefined, subversion and betrayal became the basis for the McCarthyites' new attack. In 1949 and 1950 they concentrated on the related questions of foreign policy and internal security. In this vein they first criticized Truman's appeals to bipartisanship, which, they argued, had successfully averted needed independent investigations (1) of the rationale for Roosevelt-Truman foreign policy and internal security decisions, and (2) of the adequacy of loyalty screening procedures. Then they focused on the controversial Yalta Conference agreements on Eastern Europe and China, contending that the Roosevelt and Truman administrations, by their betrayal of Eastern Europe and China, by their attempt to appease the Soviets at Yalta, Potsdam, and Teheran, and by their negligent security procedures and naiveté about communism, had contributed to the territorial and military expansion of the Soviet Union. The Eastern European and Far Eastern agreements at Yalta, they pointedly argued, dramatically confirmed communist influence on administration policy.

"Appeasement" established, the McCarthyites were able to raise the specific issue of atomic espionage after the Soviet explosion of an atomic bomb in September 1949. In much the same manner they attributed the Soviet bomb to the subversive efforts of disloyal federal employees. Even before the Rosenberg-Greenglass-Gold arrests and trial, this charge struck a responsive note, perhaps because of an American psychological dependence on atomic monopoly. By 1949 most Americans regarded this atomic monopoly as not simply control of another powerful weapon but as the one sure means of insuring peace and security. From this conviction sprang the beliefs that the atomic bomb could remain forever an exclusively American secret, and that effective internal-security procedures could prevent any other nation from acquiring the weapon. These beliefs were shattered by the announcement of the Soviet bomb, and the threat of atomic war and atomic annihilation was brought directly home to the United States. Regrettably, but all too naturally, the nation was ready for a witch hunt. All that was needed was documentation which would transform suspicion into established fact.

COUPLED WITH communist revolutionary success in China, the Pumpkin Papers and the Soviet bomb provided the immediate backdrop for the congressional conservatives to shift their attention to internal security in late 1949 and early 1950. "Communists-in-government" became the rallying cry, McCarthy provided the necessary documentation. By limiting his attack to the State Department, by citing numbers and referring to specific documents, by centering neither on radical nor reform politics but on internal security alone, McCarthy effectively refined the conservatives' earlier agitation of popular fears. McCarthy's strength derived from his ability to draw a convincing, seemingly documented explanation for the unsettling and unexpected international developments of preceding years. Although he had been elected during the conservative groundswell of 1946, McCarthy had the further advantage of not being politically identified with the conservative anti–New Deal leadership of the 80th Congress. In fact, during the 1948 contest for the Republican presidential nomination he had supported the moderate Harold Stassen over the conservatives Robert Taft and General Douglas MacArthur. Nor did his voting record reflect strict adherence to any cause: he supported certain Fair Deal measures and opposed others. Lastly, while on the attack McCarthy was able to convey a certain very convincing sincerity. Intellectually not very sophisticated, but a shrewd judge of public attitudes and temper, McCarthy's confident citation of excerpts from the loyalty reports seemed solid evidence. This, coupled with his early training as a prosecutor, made him a formidable advocate.

Recognizing that McCarthy's attack on the State Department could be effective and popular, the congressional conservatives took up his cause. But McCarthy was not indispensable to them, and, in certain respects, because of his independence, inconsistency, and crudity, was in some ways a potential liability. After February 1950 their only tangible support of McCarthy was limited to insuring that he had national forums from which to level his charges, and to defending him from administration and other criticisms. At no time did the McCarthyites share the Senator's narrow demands for the removal of subversives from the State Department or from foreign policy–making positions. When his charges became reckless and his methods suspect, threatening to discredit the McCarthyites' own tactics, they did not hesitate to challenge him.

The rift between McCarthy and leading congressional conservatives emerged in 1953 but became important only in 1954, during the famous Army-McCarthy hearings and the censure hearings of the special committee chaired by Arthur Watkins. In 1953 Senator Robert Taft, unwilling to oppose the Eisenhower administration's controversial nomination of Charles Bohlen as U.S. Ambassador to the Soviet Union, undercut McCarthy's attempt to defeat Senate confirmation. More importantly, in 1954, Senator Karl Mundt remained aloof when McCarthy openly assailed the loyalty of the Army. Other congressional conservatives would distinguish their position from McCarthy's during the 1954 special Senate committee's investigation of censure charges against him. These conservatives would not, for example, endorse McCarthy's efforts to impugn the patriotism of the Committee members, including the conservative chairman Arthur Watkins.

Although most congressional conservatives voted against the condemnation of McCarthy in 1954, they did so not out of personal loyalty but on grounds of alleged free speech and their continued commitment to the more general tactics of McCarthyism. Their objective—and it was one in which they succeeded—was to insure that any decision to condemn would be confined to McCarthy's methods, not his objectives; in defending him, they were concerned not so much with the man as with the communist and national-security issues he had raised. Throughout the debate leading to condemnation (the resolution did not refer to "censure"), the McCarthyites' real concern was that McCarthy's personal excesses not discredit the larger conservative anti-communist movement.

Essentially one of convenience from the beginning, the association of congressional conservatives with McCarthy dissolved during 1954. Yet, although these conservative Congressmen had consistently operated independently of the Senator, their fortunes were linked with his effectiveness and image. His repudiation and the changed political climate which had made it possible significantly weakened their own political future. They had remained a minority throughout the postwar decade, their resurgence deriving only from the national-security obsession of the Cold War years and Truman's loss of credibility. Once the tensions producing the Cold War waned, and a President untainted by any suspicions of partnership, indecision, or radicalism was elected, the influence of the McCarthyites had to diminish.

Before this, however, the McCarthyites were able to stymie the enactment of reform measures, undercut a critical analysis of the rationality of anti-communist international and internal-security policies, and significantly encourage the establishment of loyalty procedures which, serving to impugn radicalism, contributed to a status quo political atmosphere. In 1945 popular acceptance of New Deal democracy had provided a counterbalance to McCarthyite tactics. By 1950, however, with the intensification of the Cold War and the changed rhetoric of American politics, these tactics could no longer be considered simply as conservative politics. In fact, McCarthyism was consistent with national policy on questions both of containment and of loyalty-security. How this perspective shifted, how the definition of national priorities changed during the 1945–1950 period, is the subject of the next chapter.

3

Rhetoric and Reality:

Foreign Policy During

the Cold War

ASCRIBING THE NATION'S problems (both domestic and international) to the existence of "communists in government," McCarthyites simultaneously stimulated and derived support from the popular belief that national security was truly being threatened—and would continue to be theatened—unless a more resourceful approach than the Truman administration's was adopted. Indeed, by 1950 many Americans had come to believe that: (1) the Soviet Union had a definite strategy for the eventual communization of the world; (2) Soviet actions directly threatened the security of the United States; (3) that threat could assume the form of direct aggression or internal subversion; (4) the basic impetus to any revolutionary or radical political change was a Moscow-directed communist conspiracy; (5) superior military power was essential to achieving peace and security; (6) a diplomacy of compromise and concession was in effect a form of appeasement and betrayal; (7) American objectives were altruistic and humanitarian; (8) the United States—because omnipotent—could shape the world to conform to American ideals and principles; (9) the God-fearing United States had to triumph over godless communism; (10) international options were clear-cut and definable in terms of good versus evil; (11) the U.S. confrontation with the Soviet Union demanded not only the containment of Soviet expansion but the liberation of "enslaved peoples"; and (12) communist leaders, whether in the Soviet Union, Eastern Europe, or China, lacked a popular base of support and were thus able to remain in power only through terror and subversion.

By 1950 these beliefs had strengthened popular demands for victory over communism at home and abroad. Many Americans also believed that foreign policy could not be effective unless communist infiltration of the government was prevented by a strong internal-security program. Thus the themes of "communists in government" and "softness toward communism," though they reflected different concerns and fears, were directly linked in the public mind: victory abroad could not be secured without victory at home; a dynamic foreign policy necessitated a rigorous internal-security program.

POPULAR FEARS about threats to American national security were far indeed from being endemic in the United States at the end of World War II. In 1945, according to opinion polls, most Americans believed that a durable peace required the continuation of Allied cooperation; thus they welcomed the Yalta Conference as a means of achieving that objective. Majority opinion supported Roosevelt's efforts to promote mutual trust and understanding with the Soviet Union; it recognized the necessity for compromise and appreciated the inevitable differences in purposes between the "democracies"

of the United States, the Soviet Union, and Great Britain.
In 1945 most Americans considered the Soviet Union to be
not the Anti-Christ but a Great Power having legitimate
security aims which sometimes conflicted with those of the
United States. Most differences between the United States
and the Soviet Union were considered resolvable through international conferences—particularly conferences involving
the Big Three—and required diplomatic compromise, not
military confrontation.

In line with these views, a popular distrust of the military
prevailed. This distrust was reflected in support for limiting
the role of the military in the control and development of
atomic energy, demands for immediate demobilization of
troops, and opposition to peacetime conscription. While ap-
preciating the limits of American military power, many citizens
also recognized the important role that anti-Nazi resistance
forces and British and Soviet troops had played in the ultimate Allied victory over the Axis powers.

In short, majority opinion in America believed in neither
the omniscience nor the omnipotence of the United States;
peace and security depended on continued American cooperation with other nations, whether major or minor powers.
Finally, most Americans demanded that the administration
pursue an internationalist foreign policy—multilaterally rather
than unilaterally run. They considered economic problems
the basis of threats to world peace, and felt that these could
be settled through aid and negotiation.

By 1950 a dramatic shift in this outlook had taken place,
and it contributed to the emergence of McCarthyism. It was
a reaction that differed considerably from the conservative
reaction following World War I. The earlier Red Scare had
been a direct product of the passions and fears wrought by
American involvement in the war, and represented a distinct
domestic political conservatism. In contrast, McCarthyism

was not directly a product of the war, since it appeared not in 1945 but in 1950, nor was its thrust overtly anti-progressive. Instead it was the product of the Cold War confrontation between the United States and the Soviet Union and the resulting obsession on the part of Americans with national security. Because this confrontation was viewed not in terms of power politics but in distinctly moralistic terms, it led to no less than an oversimplified belief in the possibility of, indeed demand for, victory over the Soviet Anti-Christ.

This change in national opinion was in great part shaped by the rhetoric of the Truman administration. In the period 1945–1949—that is, before Senator McCarthy's Wheeling speech—the Truman administration conducted foreign policy debate along narrowly anti-communist lines. To secure support for its containment policy, from 1947 through 1949 administration rhetoric vastly oversimplified the choices confronting the nation; it also characterized international change in terms of crisis and national security. Indeed, the administration's anti-communist rhetoric, the thrust of its appeals both before and after McCarthy's Wheeling speech, did not differ substantively from that of McCarthy and his conservative congressional supporters.

After 1945 the Truman administration had gradually, yet distinctly, renounced the priorities of the Roosevelt administration. The bases for this shift are to be found in two dominant strains of Truman's thought: a deep distrust of Soviet objectives, and a belief in the importance of military superiority. In contrast to Roosevelt's sophisticated international approach, which relied on negotiation and détente, Truman's outlook—an outlook shaped by his World War I experience, his active participation in the American Legion, and his antipathy to the isolationism and anti-militarism of the 1930's—was based on the primacy of power in international politics. Although an avowed internationalist and advocate of peace, Truman believed that peace could best be secured through military deterrence and alliances. Unlike Roosevelt, whose distrust of the Soviet Union was mitigated by an expediential wartime alliance and an appreciation that Soviet involvement in Eastern Europe was as legitimate a security objective as United States involvement in Latin America, Truman felt that Soviet expansion merely confirmed the Soviet leaders' perfidy and imperialistic intentions, and thus must be averted.

Accordingly, Truman's "internationalism" assumed a unilateral form in which American national interests became the sole foundation for cooperation and peace. More importantly, in 1945, and increasingly after 1948, the administration tended to subordinate traditional diplomatic or economic options to its overriding commitment to attaining superior military power. In contrast to Roosevelt's view that disagreement, even conflict, between the United States and the Soviet Union was inevitable—and possibly even salutary, insuring a diverse world order—Truman made his administration's long-term goal the achievement of "freedom" and "democracy" for the peoples of Eastern Europe, the Soviet Union, China, and the underdeveloped world. He characterized the U.S.-Soviet conflict in moralistic terms, seeing America's role as a "mission," and redefining "appeasement" to mean the failure of the United States to confront revolutionary or disruptive change head on. A sense of American omnipotence, the belief that the United States could impose its will on the postwar world, was behind the Truman administration's rhetoric on foreign policy.

Yet this shift away from Roosevelt's foreign policy developed gradually. The 1952 priorities of the Truman administration differed radically from its 1945 priorities. This shift resulted in part from Soviet actions in Eastern Europe and the United Nations, in part from the administration's reassessment of basic foreign policy questions. What would have been politically feasible in 1945 had become politically impossible by 1952, for by then the administration, trapped in its own rhetoric, could no longer even suggest that any Soviet interest in peace or negotiation was valid.

୨◗

WHEN Harry S. Truman became President of the United States on April 12, 1945, he was faced with the immediate responsibilities of concluding the war and negotiating a settlement with the Soviet Union. Roosevelt had dominated national politics since 1932; he was the unquestioned leader of Congress and of the Democratic party, and he personified reform in the public mind. These factors, coupled with Roosevelt's personal direction of American foreign policy during the war, the nature of Truman's selection as Vice-President, and his elevation to the presidency (an unknown, uninformed former Senator acceding to the office two and a half months after his inauguration as Vice-President)—all helped to heighten Truman's political difficulties in succeeding FDR.

Having been elected on the Roosevelt ticket, Truman was in principle bound by Roosevelt's earlier commitments and decisions. At best he could revise or alter the direction of policy, but he was hardly in a position to set America off on a whole new course—at least not in the early months of his presidency, when he was overwhelmed by the responsibilities of his office and the problems of his succession.

In early 1945 Truman told the American public that he would fulfill Roosevelt's intentions in foreign policy. In his first public speech after taking the oath of office, and again when first addressing a joint session of Congress, Truman spelled out his administration's objectives in essentially

Rooseveltian terms: a commitment to international organization as the means to preserve peace, and an emphasis on the need for mutual understanding and continued postwar allied cooperation. Despite this common rhetoric, Truman's policy did differ from Roosevelt's in both priorities and methods. That is, Truman significantly qualified his reference to international cooperation and mutual understanding with the statement that real security depended on a peace based on "law" and "justice."

This reference to law and justice reflected the increased influence on policy of certain men in the State Department, the White House staff, the military, and the Cabinet. Specifically, chief among these men were James Byrnes, James Forrestal, Tom Clark, George Marshall, Dean Acheson, William Clayton, Joseph Grew, Bernard Baruch, Lucius Clay, Clark Clifford, John Snyder, William Leahy, and W. Averell Harriman. These men had played no dominant role during the war because Roosevelt shared neither their excessive Russophobia nor their military orientation, or because, in some instances, they were Truman appointees. Yet Truman, who had not been involved in forming—and lacked the requisite understanding of—Roosevelt's important foreign policy decisions, felt compelled to rely on these men for advice. Given his own feelings of inadequacy, his respect for their expertise, and his sympathy for their antipathy toward the Soviet Union, Truman's dependence on these men in itself insured a marked shift in administration policy.

The identification of security with law and justice added a new dimension to administration policy toward the Soviet occupation of Eastern Europe. To Truman, the Yalta Declaration on Liberated Europe had provided for free and democratic elections supervised equally by the United States, Great Britain, and the Soviet Union. This interpretation of the vaguely worded declaration ignored, however, both military and political realities and the "spheres of influence" agreement concluded in October 1944 by Churchill and Stalin and tacitly acceded to by Roosevelt in the armistice agreements with Rumania, Hungary, and Bulgaria. Most importantly, Truman's interpretation overlooked the declaration's unanimous-consent provision concerning the operation of the tripartite Allied Control Commission; by permitting a Soviet veto, this provision in effect ensured that the Soviet military occupation role would be a controlling one (like what had occurred in Italy, where British-U.S. military occupation had precluded the Soviets having any role whatsoever). Moreover, in view of the Soviets' strategic interest in having "friendly" governments on her borders and her expressed commitment to prevent the re-establishment, as in 1919, of a Western *cordon sanitaire,* absolutely free elections (free, that is, of Soviet intervention or pressure) were impossible for Eastern Europe. Nor was Truman's commitment to free elections in Eastern Europe wholly consistent; Truman was willing, after all, to recognize the Argentine government and to tolerate British and French colonialism. In reality, the conflict over "free elections" and "justice" for Eastern Europe masked the administration's principal concern: the extension of Soviet influence in that area.

Although the administration held to its commitment, it formally hoped to avoid a complete break with the Soviet Union. At the same time, it quelled popular fears that a provocative policy would frustrate a lasting peace. Adopting a moralistic rhetoric that stressed specific commitments and abstract principles (as opposed to more real nationalistic or strategic considerations), the administration attempted to project an altruistic, noninterventionist position. In its rhetoric it pointedly sought to capture popular suspicions about Soviet restrictions on individual liberties, and ignored the fundamental questions of whether American principles of

justice necessarily had universal validity and whether their
application to Eastern Europe and not Latin America or
European colonial areas reflected a double standard. In effect
this rhetoric served to increase popular anti-communism without substantively altering the international situation. An
October 11, 1946, statement of Acting Secretary of State
Dean Acheson to the press on the occasion of the Yugoslavian
government's trial and conviction of Roman Catholic Arch-
bishop Stepinac made plain this shift in administration emphasis:

> It is the civil liberties aspect of this thing [the Stepinac
> trial] which causes us concern, aspects which raise questions
> as to whether the trial has any implications looking toward
> the impairment of freedom of religion or worship. . . .
> You [the press] will recall that under the Constitution
> and laws of the United States, fairness of trial is guaranteed
> under the 14th Amendment and the Supreme Court of the
> United States has set aside as not being legal procedure at
> all, trials in which the courtroom has been dominated by
> feelings adverse to the defendant by demonstrations of
> prejudice. That is deeply inherent in the American system,
> that the very essence of due process of law is that in trials
> we shall lean over backwards in being fair to the defendant,
> in the atmosphere in the court room, in forbidding demon-
> strations of spectators, in opportunity of facing and cross-
> examining witnesses—all these matters seem to be absolutely
> inherent in the matter of a fair trial.

In a related sense, throughout 1945 the Truman administration, while publicly expressing support for Roosevelt's
policy of accommodation, behind the scenes sought to limit
the extension of Soviet influence. This objective underlay
both the sharp exchange between President Truman and
Soviet Foreign Minister Molotov over Soviet policy in Poland
in April and the abrupt U.S. termination of lend-lease in
May. It was also a factor in the administration's revision of
earlier German occupation and reparations policy (notably

JCS 1067*), specifically its attempts to promote German political and economic recovery. As early as May 12, 1945, the commitment to implementing the Yalta Far Eastern agreements was being re-evaluated by the administration.

Fearing that the give and take of diplomacy would necessitate the acceptance of a dominant postwar Soviet role, and that only U.S. economic and military strength might prevent this, at Potsdam Truman adopted a rigid, uncompromising stance. He preferred to postpone agreement should the Soviets not accept American terms. This strategy of postponement was also intended to minimize postwar Soviet influence in the occupied areas; by keeping the situation fluid it was hoped that subsequent economic and political pressure would ensure Soviet military withdrawal from Eastern Europe and the Balkans.

§●

ALTHOUGH THE successful development and demonstration of the atomic bomb in 1945 seemed to provide the administration with a new and effective bargaining level in negotiations with the Soviet Union, possession of the bomb could not destroy Soviet influence in Eastern Europe or Asia. Nor could possession of the bomb be openly used to pressure the Soviet Union to agree to administration views; in 1945 neither

---

* A directive drafted on September 22, 1944, by the Joint Chiefs of Staff concerning the dismantling or destruction of German war plants and limiting German industrial productivity as the basis for preventing the re-emergence of an aggressive power. JCS 1067 was vaguely worded and unilateral in intent; it was drafted without consultation with the Soviet Union or Great Britain, and its economic provisions were entirely discretionary in avoiding specific figures and criteria. Although the directive was not formally repudiated and was the subject of an intensive policy examination, increasingly during 1945 the administration sought to minimize its aim to deter German economic recovery.

American nor international public opinion would have countenanced that tactic. Cognizant of these limitations, the administration sought to contain Russia by shows of sizable conventional force.

This maneuver required that the administration disregard current popular demands for the immediate demobilization of American troops and the dismantling of those bases acquired from Japan. In fact, both the War and Navy Departments went so far as to urge Congress to enact universal military training. Universal military training, they argued, was democratic in principle; by making possible a strong standing army, it would ensure security and preserve the peace. Moreover, it was consistent with Roosevelt's last State of the Union address (January 6, 1945).

A statement of May 26, 1945, by Secretary of the Navy James Forrestal, never released because of White House fears of misinterpretation, combined Forrestal's own peculiar historical vision with the prevailing assumptions of the military on international affairs. Forrestal observed that:

1. The evidence of twentieth-century history, the inter-relationship of the nature of the world, and the position of the United States therein, demonstrate that:
   a. There is every likelihood that any war involving one or more major powers will develop into a world war.
   b. There is little likelihood that the United States can escape eventual involvement in a world war.
2. The evidence of history also indicates that:
   a. If adequate force is applied in sufficient time against aggressor nations, incipient world wars will not materialize and vast expenditures of American lives and treasure will be avoided.
   b. If world wars should materialize, through absence of preventive measures, immediate and overpowering action by the United States armed forces will greatly lessen the expenditure of American lives and treasure that otherwise would be involved.

Truman knew that in 1945 the public would not be receptive to these arguments. It was distrustful of armaments programs, viewing any militarist course as provoking tensions and frustrating peace. Most Americans preferred diplomacy to arms, in part because they sustained a deep hope in the promise of the United Nations. To secure universal military training Truman had to convince the public of the peaceful purpose of military power. First of all, he defended the U.S. decision to maintain military bases on the grounds that they provided protection against future wars and were thus consistent with the United Nations Charter. In addresses to Congress on October 23 and December 19, 1945, Truman extolled the importance for world peace and national security of both universal military training and a strong defense program. He suggested that the failure to implement these measures would result in war; disarmament, he claimed, would frustrate peace. "Urgent" congressional action at the "earliest possible moment" was necessary insofar as

all nations—and particularly those unfortunate nations which have felt the heel of the Nazis, the Fascists or the Japs—know that the desire for peace is futile unless there is enough strength ready and willing to enforce that desire in an emergency. Among the things that have encouraged aggression and the spread of war in the past have been the unwillingness of the United States realistically to face the fact, and her refusal to fortify her arms of peace before the forces of aggression could gather in strength. It [the future of world peace] will depend upon whether or not the United States is willing to maintain the physical strength necessary to act as a safeguard against any future aggressor.

Although the administration's 1945 efforts to secure congressional approval of universal military training failed, it was not resigned to this rebuff. Recognizing prevalent popular suspicions about the military, on December 19, 1946, Truman appointed a special presidential commission, headed by Karl Compton, president of the Massachusetts Institute of Technology, and composed of prominent civilians from the academic, professional, judicial, and business communities, to evaluate the nation's military needs.* The commission members were selected to ensure a definite civilian, rather than military, image, and to create the appearance of an impartial expert study. A November 13, 1945, memo from Truman to Secretary of War Robert Patterson highlighted the President's public relations objective: the commission, Truman wrote, would show the country that "we have thoroughly in mind the educational, welfare and civilian aspects of our training program."

After prolonged deliberation the commission recommended, in its report of May 29, 1947, congressional approval of universal training; its report stressed the gravity of the world situation and the necessity of a large standing army to preserve the peace. In addition, the commission concluded that all practical steps must be taken to safeguard the religious, moral, educational, and recreational welfare of armed services personnel. Truman was more than pleased by this report, describing it before a special conference with editors of business and trade papers as "the most satisfactory and sane report that has been made public." †

* Other commission members included Joseph E. Davies, lawyer and former ambassador; Daniel Poling, clergyman; Samuel Rosenman, jurist and former special counsel to President Roosevelt; Anna Rosenberg, public and industrial relations consultant; Truman Gibson, lawyer and former civilian aide to the Secretary of War; Harold Dodds, president of Princeton University; Edmund Walsh, vice-president of Georgetown University; and Charles Wilson, president of General Electric.

† The report, though partially undercutting popular suspicions of a military program, did not secure congressional approval. Indeed, only in 1948 did Congress, influenced by the crisis atmosphere produced by the Berlin blockade and Czechoslovakian coup, enact a peacetime conscription program. Even then, Congress approved only a selective and not a universal service system.

BECAUSE HE WAS convinced that the nation could pursue an effective diplomacy only from a position of superior military strength, Truman also had little faith in the value of summit conferences to resolve differences between the United States and the Soviet Union. Nonetheless, after Potsdam he encountered persistent pressure from the press and the public for his views on another Big Three meeting. Truman's initial response to this pressure was evasive or noncommittal. At times he suggested that the existence of the United Nations made a conference unnecessary; at other times he expressed interest in a conference, but only if it were held in the United States. A summit conference, he went on to argue, should not be convened unless the participants were assured it would be meaningful. This assurance required that a program delineating areas of agreement be drawn up as an advance condition of any conference.

By 1948, however, Truman was openly expressing opposition to the very idea of summit diplomacy. He justified his position on grounds of Soviet untrustworthiness and bad faith. The Russians often concluded agreements, he said, only to violate them when they found it convenient to do so. Truman further characterized the Soviet bargaining position as inflexible and unreasonable; the Russians, in his view, would conclude agreements only on their own terms.

Warning against an undue reliance on the negotiating process, Truman counseled the public not to fall victim to the "insidious propaganda that peace can be attained solely by wanting peace." The public must realize, he argued in defense of the Truman Doctrine on May 13, 1947, that the Russians "understand one language [force] and that is the language they are going to get from this point."

Truman reiterated these sentiments in an April 23, 1948, conference with business and trade newspaper editors, and

contrasted U.S. virtue to Soviet perfidy, noting that the
United States sought only peace and what is "right," while
the Soviet Union was expansionist and believed that force
counts for everything. Assailing the interest in peace on the
part of Stalin and the "other crackpots on this side of the
water," Truman cited Roosevelt's and his own wartime efforts
to reach a negotiated understanding with the Soviets at Yalta
and Potsdam. These diplomatic conferences, Truman observed, had subsequently been frustrated by Soviet violations
of agreements presumably concluded in good faith. Only
when the United States had the military ability to enforce
agreement, Truman argued, could peace be secured. In this
same vein he observed that his efforts in 1945 to secure peace
had been frustrated by domestic pressures for rapid American
troop demobilization—and at a time when the Soviet Union
retained four million men under arms.

By 1949 Truman disparaged any suggestion of further
summit diplomacy or indeed compromise on U.S.-Soviet differences. He contended that to engage in either would be to
ignore international realities. In order for such negotiations
tangibly to minimize U.S.-Soviet differences, Truman claimed,
the United States would have to "give" Berlin, Korea,
Germany, Japan, and East Asia to the Russians. On the
other hand, he confidently predicted that the administration's
confrontation approach (which he described as a "war of
nerves"), relying on military strength and refusing concessions in the interest simply of reaching agreement, would
finally result in "surrender" and peace. He would "raise the
Iron Curtain by peaceful means." During the early 1950's
Truman continued to oppose convening a conference to work
out U.S.-Soviet differences or initiate discussions on disarmament by again impugning Soviet objectives; he added
that the timing for such a conference was not propitious. A
significant solution could be reached, he maintained, only
through the deterrent force of superior American power,

which had not yet been attained, and the Soviet Union's realization that her aggressive aims could not be achieved.

By 1950 the thrust of administration rhetoric expressed the need to confront the communist threat directly; it depicted the Soviet-American conflict in moralistic terms, refusing to concede either the legitimacy of Soviet objectives or the self-seeking strategy of American ones. While the administration justified the American military build-up as self-defense, it deplored the Soviet build-up as aggressive and belligerent. It criticized Stalin's efforts to extend the Soviet sphere of influence in Asia and Europe, but it proclaimed that such American efforts as lifting "the Iron Curtain by peaceful means" or protesting the Yugoslavian government's failure to adhere to American constitutional guarantees in its judicial proceedings were purely disinterested, noninterventionist, and internationalist. The effect of this rhetoric was cumulative; by the late 1940's the administration had managed to circumvent popular aversion to the confrontation course, which was essentially one of relying on military strength to limit Soviet influence. More importantly, by successfully discrediting the value of negotiations, the possibility of a rational discussion of policy alternatives was foreclosed.

THE ADMINISTRATION'S ATTEMPTS to limit Russian influence were, to be sure, strongly influenced by postwar developments in Europe. The war had shattered the economies and undermined the political stability of Western Europe, while the German retreat in the face of the Soviet offensive had made Soviet occupation and control of Eastern Europe possible. The dismemberment of Germany had created a power vacuum which further enhanced Soviet influence on the Continent. To redress this power imbalance and to remove the causes of disorder and chaos in Western Europe, the

Truman administration initially relied upon America's economic resources. By a loan to the British government, it attempted to insure Britain's continuing role as a countervailing power in the Mediterranean, in the Middle East, and in Asia. Similarly, by helping to restore economic stability in Western Europe and in Greece, it hoped to undercut the political strength of the national Communist parties. Although in fact there were motives in power politics for this economic aid, administration rhetoric maintained that humanitarianism and economic self-interest were the primary objectives involved.

In pressing Congress to ratify a loan to Great Britain in late 1945, Truman contended that the United States had a moral responsibility to the British because of their wartime sacrifices and losses. He further maintained that a multilateral trading system was essential for postwar prosperity, both at home and abroad, arguing that the U.S. had to avoid the prewar protective tariff and trade policies that had contributed to the Great Depression. Once Congress had approved the loan, Truman continued to deny that this "agreement between the United States and Great Britain [was] directed against any other country." The United States, he said, sought only to promote trade with all countries; the preference for Britain was based on the special circumstances wrought by wartime destruction.

This economic thrust of U.S. foreign policy, and its attendant altruistic and internationalist rationale, constituted the administration's justifications in 1946 and 1947 for other major policy decisions. In recommending U.S. military aid to Latin America on May 6, 1946, and on May 26, 1947, Truman specifically denied that this aid would contribute to an arms race or lead to indiscriminately subsidizing the military of other countries. His administration, Truman affirmed, did not intend to cede weapons of war to those who might use them "to oppose the peaceful and democratic principles to which the United States and other American nations have so often subscribed." He added:

> In executing this program it will be borne in mind, more-over, that it is the policy of this Government to encourage the establishment of sound economic conditions in the other American republics. . . . Operations under the proposed legislation will be conducted with full and constant aware-ness that no encouragement should be given to the imposi-tion upon other people of any useless burden of armaments which could handicap the economic improvement which all countries so strongly desire.

Truman also emphasized economic themes in his January 6, 1947, State of the Union address. Citing domestic pros-perity as his administration's main objective, he argued that it could not be attained without a high level of international trade; he also noted the importance of a sound domestic economy to an effective foreign policy. For both domestic and internationalist reasons, therefore, the President asserted that his administration had the postwar responsibility of re-ducing tariff barriers and supporting the reconstruction of war-torn economies. He then qualified an acknowledgment of disagreement between the United States and Soviet Union by saying, "Whatever differences there may have been between us and the Soviet Union, however, should not be allowed to obscure the fact that the basic interests of both nations lie in the early making of peace under which the peoples of all countries may return, as free men and women, to the essential tasks of production and reconstruction."

Despite this rhetoric, the administration was less concerned with economic aid itself than with the ways that aid might affect Soviet influence in Europe. In fact, it was precisely because of this concern with security that the administration offered military aid to the Greek and Turkish governments when the British decided to withdraw theirs. While the ad-ministration feared the strategic implications of a total withdrawal of Western support, it also feared that the American public and Congress might fail to appreciate the need to support the established Greek and Turkish governments.

Thus to Joseph Jones, State Department aide, the general European situation required a vigorous administration program to "inform the public and convince the Congress adequately with respect to today's crisis." Jones urged a full description of the "dangers"—essentially, Russian dangers—and future costs of the failure to supply economic aid. In a February 26, 1947, memo to William Benton, Jones wrote:

> If these areas [Britain and her Empire, France, Greece and China] are allowed to spiral downward into economic anarchy, then at best they will drop out of the U.S. orbit and try an independent nationalistic policy; at worst they will swing into the Russian orbit.
> We will then face the world alone. What will then be the cost, in dollars and cents, of our armaments and of our economic isolation? I do not see how we could possibly avoid a depression far greater than that of 1929–1932 and crushing taxes to pay for the direct commitments we would be forced to make around the world.

Assistant Secretary of State William Clayton, in a memo of March 5 urging the administration to embark upon a "shock" campaign to convince the American public that the gravity of the world situation required immediate American action, more pointedly identified the problem as one resulting from the Soviet Union's subversive efforts to capitalize on economic distress and "bore from within." Clayton added:

> The reins of world leadership are fast slipping from Britain's competent but now very weak hands.
> These reins will be picked up either by the United States or by Russia. If by Russia, there will almost certainly be a war in the next decade or so, with the odds against us. If by the United States, war can almost certainly be prevented.

Clayton and Jones perceived the issue confronting the

United States to be world leadership, though neither was an idealist or internationalist. Both men equally deplored the "subversive" character of any reduction of Western influence or any radical political change. To insure support for economic-military aid, they had to convince the public and Congress of the seriousness of this crisis. To cut away public and congressional indifference, they thus suggested their "domino theory" of international politics—that should Greece and Turkey "fall," the whole Middle East would be "lost"; that should the Middle East "fall," France would "capitulate" with the resultant "loss" of Western Europe and North Africa, and so on down the line. A redefinition of Soviet subversion and aggression was also needed since, in the absence of a direct Soviet move, the public and Congress might not be shaken out of their apathy.

It was left to Truman to accomplish these goals in his dramatic March 12, 1947, address to a specially convened joint session of Congress. Out of this address emerged the so-called Truman Doctrine; its tone was alarmist, its content crisis-oriented, and its analysis vastly oversimplified. Truman maintained that the fate of Greece and Turkey would determine the future course of world politics. Should Greece and Turkey "fall," he said, the fortunes of neighboring European and Middle Eastern states would be profoundly, indeed irreversibly, affected. The imposition of totalitarian regimes in Greece and Turkey would undermine the foundations of world peace and hence adversely affect the U.S. national security.

Addressing himself to the civil conflict in Greece, Truman did not uncritically defend the royalist government. He conceded the imperfections of the Greek monarchy, but argued that as a democratic nation the United States must provide the Greek people with the opportunity to progress toward freedom and democracy within their existing political institutions. The basic premise of U.S. policy, Truman contended, must therefore be to help "free" peoples resist attempts at subjugation by "armed minorities" or "outside pressure."

Although he emphasized the revolutionary aspects of the Greek situation and argued that the threat to freedom in Greece (and indirectly to the United States) was posed by armed guerrillas "led" by communists, in 1947 Truman did not formally recommend U.S. military intervention. Nor did he suggest that the basic thrust of American policy be military. Finally, although his reference to "outside pressure" implied that the revolutionaries were supported by the Russians, he did not directly name them as the aggressor. Instead he defined the revolution as the result of economic distress—a combination of underdevelopment and the destruction created by the war. Accordingly, he urged Congress to approve a program of economic aid and technical assistance. By bolstering the Greek economy, Truman argued, the threat of "subversive" exploitation inherent in economic misery and political chaos would be undercut.

By thus identifying the factors that had led to the civil war largely in economic terms, Truman was able to maintain that the "subversive" efforts could be defeated by American economic aid alone. He conceded that the guerrilla movement— "led" by communists—posed a military threat to the legitimate Greek government, but he characterized that movement as a dissident minority with little indigenous support. Confident that economic, as opposed to military, aid would succeed, he insisted that:

> The internal construction and the restoration to a peacetime economy is what we are principally interested in, on a free basis. . . . My idea is the restoration of a peacetime economy in these countries [Greece and Turkey], with the hope that they will inaugurate a free government that will be for the benefit of the people.

Such arguments constituted the administration's rationale for an interventionist policy involving United States support for essentially undemocratic governments. Concerned over the possibility of an adverse public reaction, the President emphatically denied that independent United States aid to Greece and Turkey was contrary to America's commitment to the United Nations. The critical nature of the Greek situation, he explained, required that the administration bypass the United Nations. The Truman Doctrine, he maintained, would actually strengthen the United Nations, since the United States, by aiding the Greek and Turkish governments, would provide tangible evidence of her intention to accept her internationalist responsibilities and her commitment to the integrity of small but independent states. Presenting his administration's policy in a moralistic light, he claimed that the United States had no territorial or political ambitions in offering this aid, but was motivated solely by a desire for world peace. Such rhetoric tended to strengthen popular beliefs that the American attitude was peaceful; that American support of the Greek monarchy in the civil war was not interventionist; and that American unilateral action was consistent with the internationalist principles of the United Nations Charter.

After congressional approval of the Greek-Turkish aid bill, however, the administration dramatically changed its rationale. In a special message to Congress on the implementation of the aid program, Truman pointedly called the Greek guerrilla movement an alien one "subservient to foreign influence from which it draws support." Although the communist guerrillas were numerically only a small minority, Truman observed, they nevertheless hoped to disrupt the Greek economy and terrorize village life in order to make the Greeks more receptive to communist ideology. "Owing to Communist obstruction," he maintained, the economic recovery of Greece would have to be postponed until internal security had been re-established, for "only" when the warfare against the guerrillas had been successfully concluded could an economic program be effective. In a final admonition, Truman warned that should "outside aid" to the guerrillas increase, a new American response might be required.

Thus by 1948 the administration's reaction to communist activity in Greece had not very subtly shifted from economic encouragement to military aid. Underlying this new approach was the contention that a revolutionary threat had to be confronted militarily, not economically; that it derived its influence from terror and alien support, not underdevelopment or the destruction of war. As redefined by the administration, the threat of revolution came not from overt aggression by foreign-controlled movements but from subversion on the part of native radicals committed to an alien ideology. According to this view, revolutions were capable of being externally initiated and controlled. Truman's emphasis on the numerical weakness and dependence of the revolutionaries on a foreign power provided a convincing justification for an American military response.

Depicting American economic or military intervention as no more than a response to foreign aggression, Truman strengthened the belief that the application of American resources, if accompanied by the necessary will and resolve, could successfully prevent any untoward developments in the postwar world. This rhetoric, intended only to justify American aid to the royalist government of Greece, inadvertently served to create a mode of reasoning by which the administration's own larger policies came to be judged. In fact, it was by just such reasoning that the popular belief that the administration had "lost" China came about. If radical revolutions were foreign-inspired and lacked indigenous popular support; if the national security required an American response to every "alien-directed subversion"; and if, furthermore, the United States, through the effective use of economic-military resources, could avert "subversive" threats to "democratic" governments, then—so went this reasoning—

the Truman administration could and indeed should have acted to check the Communist takeover in China.

๑

THE SAME ATTITUDE toward communist subversion constituted the administration's rationale for the Marshall Plan. Western Europe's major postwar economic problems, which resulted from wartime destruction, German occupation, a succession of poor harvests, and Soviet obstruction of normal European trade relations, had brought about a politics of insecurity and instability. Native Communist parties, particularly in France and Italy, had dramatically increased their strength by exploiting these politics.

Although the Truman administration, and in particular the State Department, was gravely worried about the French and Italian situations, there was some doubt that they could convince Congress and the public to share their apprehensions. For one thing, the debate over the Truman Doctrine had revealed latent opposition to administration "internationalism" from both liberals and conservatives. Liberals mainly opposed the doctrine's underlying military orientation and, along with it, the administration's decision to bypass the United Nations. Conservatives opposed the economic costs of the Greek-Turkish aid program and, implicit in it, the commitment to an extended American overseas role. The administration thus hesitated to propose a further aid program for Western Europe until Congress had approved 'the Truman Doctrine. Yet in public statements as well as in private planning preceding Secretary of State George C. Marshall's Harvard University address calling for the Marshall Plan, the State Department did seek to enlighten the public on the significance of the European situation for the United States. In private discussions on the tactics essential to ensuring that enlightenment, the department decided that the military

orientation of the Truman Doctrine had to be played down
and its positive, or economic, aspects highlighted. In a May
20 memo to department personnel, Joseph Jones specifically
recommended that Secretary Marshall make a major address
rebutting domestic and foreign "misrepresentations" of the
Truman Doctrine as militaristic anti-communism.

> The indications of suspicion and skepticism with which
> foreign peoples are beginning to view American aid are
> alarming, and it would seem to be of first importance to
> spell out our design for reconstruction and to give a positive
> concept upon which peoples of Europe essentially can rally
> and upon which they can pin their hopes. . . . We have a
> great deal to gain by convincing the world that we have
> something positive and attractive to offer, and not just anti-
> Communism.

To this end, Marshall's June 5 speech emphasized America's
responsibilities of world leadership and its need to adopt a
positive economic program for resolving the problems of
Western Europe. Stressing the seriousness and "enormous
complexity" of the European economic situation, Marshall
identified the source of the problem as the "dislocation"
brought about by the requirements of war and the war's
destruction. The European economic crisis, Marshall said,
affected American economic interests and thus required an
American response. Warning against the intrusion of partisan
passions and prejudices into the domestic debate about
possible responses, Marshall further stated:

> Our policy is directed not against any country or doc-
> trine but against hunger, poverty, desperation, and chaos.
> . . . Any government that is willing to assist in the task of
> recovery will find full cooperation . . . on the part of the
> United States Government. Any government which ma-
> neuvers to block the recovery cannot expect help from us.
> . . . The role of this country should consist of friendly aid
> in the drafting of such a program so far as it may be
> practical for us to do so.

In contrast to Marshall's quietly analytic address, Truman's subsequent appeals—in public statements, press conferences, and specific recommendations to Republican congressional leaders—were all much more crisis-oriented and covertly anti-Soviet in emphasizing national security and the U.S. responsibility to safeguard freedom, or in representing Europe's shakiness as a problem of subversion. Indeed, in his address recommending the Marshall Plan to Congress, Truman warned:

> Rapid changes are taking place in Europe which affect our foreign and national security. There is an increasing threat to nations which are striving to maintain a form of government which grants freedom to its citizens. The United States is deeply concerned with the survival of freedom in those nations. It is of vital importance that we act now.

Because of the "gravity" and "critical" nature of the French and Italian situations, Truman further argued, both nations could fall should the United States not provide "immediate" aid. The alternative to aid was to leave the "Iron Curtain at the Atlantic Ocean." Should this come about, the United States would have no option, Truman declared, but "to move out completely and prepare for War." On the other hand, he quickly added, should the United States provide economic aid, this ominous development of subversion by "political groups" could be averted. The "urgent" and "critical" nature of the situation, Truman concluded, therefore required the "immediate" convening of the Appropriations and Foreign Policy Committees of both houses so that Congress could consider and (presumably) approve the administration's economic aid measure "at the earliest practicable time." Once again Truman's rhetoric only served to intensify popular fears about the Russians. His stress on American altruism and nobility gave moral legitimacy to what was an interventionist, unilateral approach to foreign policy, and his emphasis on both the uniqueness of these crises and communism's lack of indigenous popular support made direct confrontation seem the only way to insure a stable world that was both pro-American and peaceful. Inaction was appeasement, and appeasement could only lead to a disastrous world war.

$\vartheta\!\!\blacktriangleright$

ALTHOUGH THE BASIS for Truman's 1947 remarks had been the State Department's recommended economic approach to foreign affairs, by mid-1948 the administration was stressing the need for a more effective military policy in Europe. Lumping together the recent *coup* in Czechoslovakia, Soviet pressure on the Finnish government, civil war in Greece, and the real chance of a Communist electoral victory in Italy, Truman charged that the Soviet Union and "its agents" were committed to destroying the freedom and independence of those countries. While conceding that the economic recovery of Europe had to be assured, Truman further argued that the European states should also be provided with the means of protecting themselves against both internal and external aggression. Specifically, he praised and expressed full U.S. support for the Brussels Pact, which he believed thoroughly consistent with the principles of the United Nations Charter and the cause of world peace.

At the same time, the administration renewed its efforts to secure congressional enactment of universal military training. Its spokesmen persistently emphasized the gravity of the world crisis, the necessity for "immediate" action, and the propriety of a policy that relied on military strength. Peace, Truman argued, could best be secured through superior military strength; he disparaged both traditional diplomacy and the historic American opposition to a strong military. The President developed these arguments in a letter to former Secretary of War Robert Patterson, then chairman of the

National Security Committee, a private citizens' group supporting peacetime conscription:

> The National Security Committee is doing a valuable service to the American people in reminding them once again of the urgent need for universal military training in the country today. I pray that your efforts will be successful.
>
> The purpose which led me to recommend to the Congress the enactment of a universal training law was the preservation of peace. The future peace of the world can be threatened only by an aggressor tempted by the prospect of an easy conquest. . . . Adequate measures of national security . . . are the one sure means of putting a stop sign on the road that leads to world aggression.
>
> While it cannot stand alone, universal training is the surest single measure that we can take to serve notice on potential aggressors that the country is prepared—and determined—to defend its freedom.
>
> . . . May God save us from a final catastrophic conflict by granting our democracy the strength and wisdom to secure enduring peace through adequate preparedness now.

In a St. Patrick's Day address in 1948, Truman openly identified the Soviet Union as the primary source of potential aggression in the contemporary world. In so doing he established an essentially bipolar framework for international politics. Soviet "agents," Truman argued, were fighting in Greece, working to subvert the freedom of Italy, and attempting to undermine domestic support for a strong American defense program. Those who opposed that program, he said, were deceiving the public and weakening the country. He then went on to contrast the false, atheistic doctrine of communist progress with the morally upright nature of American defense policy:

> The United States has become the principal protector of the free world.
>
> To carry out that responsibility we must maintain our strength—military, economic and moral. . . .
>
> We must beware of those who are devoting themselves

to sowing the seeds of disunity among our people. . . .

We must not fall victim to the insidious propaganda that peace can be obtained solely by wanting peace. This theory is advanced in the hope that it will deceive our people and that we will permit our strength to dwindle because of the false belief that all is well in the world. . . .

We must not be confused about the issue which confronts the world today. . . . It is tyranny and freedom. . . .

And even worse, communism denies the very existence of God. Religion is persecuted because it stands for freedom under God. This threat to our liberty and to our faith must be faced by each one of us. . . .

In the end, the oversimplified moralism of this rhetoric was to effectively reduce the administration's own political maneuverability. If confrontation was the only means to fulfill a holy mission, and if, in addition, the nation's major adversary was wholly evil, then to compromise or counsel restraint was not merely immoral but impolitic. Since only a loss of faith, a weakness of purpose, or a lack of vision could impede America's attaining victory, and since the Soviet threat was represented as being essentially subversive and not the result of international strategic realities, Truman's rhetoric buttressed a popular belief in American omnipotence. If it chose, or so the thread of this rhetoric ran, the United States could impose its principles on the world. This being the case, the country's main problem was less the Soviet Union than the will, purpose, and wisdom of the American people and their government.

These arguments came to the fore in 1949 when the administration sought congressional and public support for the ratification of the North Atlantic Treaty Organization (NATO). The administration stressed the defensive, internationalist, and strategic purposes of the proposed alliance. In effect, Truman argued that the American military program was simply a defensive response to both Soviet "manipulation of the conspiratorial activities of the world communist movement" and the size and aggressive purposes of Soviet land armies. In the absence of a strong Western army, Truman contended, war was inevitable. To support this contention, he specifically attributed the outbreak of World Wars I and II to the U.S. failure to remain armed and accept international responsibilities. The Cold War, he said, resulted from the forced demobilization of American troops in 1945 and Congress' subsequent failure to enact universal military training. The security of the United States and indeed future world peace would be gravely threatened if the U.S. failed to conclude the NATO alliance.

Moralistic arguments were also pressed into service: the U.S.-Soviet confrontation was a conflict between good and evil, between Christian democracy and atheistic communism, between freedom and totalitarianism. The greatest obstacle to peace, Truman contended, stemmed from a "modern tyranny led by a small group who have abandoned their faith in God. . . . Our effort to resist and overcome this tyranny is essentially a moral effort." Developing these themes in an address on December 21, 1949, Truman asserted:

> If man could achieve self-government and kinship with his God throughout the world, peace would not tremble in the constant dread of war. . . . If we could mobilize world opinion among all men who walk the earth, there would never be another war.
>
> This we cannot do alone. For the earth is deeply divided between free and captive peoples. There is no appeal to the brotherhood of men who live in deadly fear of the concentration camp. Until the captive peoples of the world emerge from darkness, they cannot see the hand we hold out in friendship. While they are made to respond to our handclasp with a mailed fist, we have no choice but to stand ready in self-defense.
>
> Much as we prize peace and friendship, we prize freedom more. And much as we trust in God, while He is rejected by

so many in the world, we must trust in ourselves. In an age when peace must be protected, we must resort to our own strength to hold aggression at bay.

Thus the administration represented a highly complex political-military problem in the essentially simplistic format of a morality play. The persistent evocation of moral themes strengthened the view of Soviet objectives as being entirely conspiratorial and created an emotional atmosphere wherein any change on the international scene became an immediate threat to American security. By 1949 the administration affirmed that the Soviet threat could only be undercut militarily, either by strengthening the nation's armed forces or providing military aid to "peace-loving," "democratic" nations—or, preferably, both. As the administration chose to view the European situation, military action became the only rational solution. It went further in offering the confident assurance, should the public support its military policy, of an eventual and complete American victory over communism.

THE TRUMAN ADMINISTRATION'S rationale for Point IV, its technical assistance program to underdeveloped countries, contrasted the same themes of American altruism and internationalism to Soviet expansionism and interventionism. As stated, the purpose of Point IV was twofold: to promote stability (American altruism) and to avert revolution (communist subversion). Its underlying premise was that undesirable political change could be averted by an American commitment to technical assistance. To enlist support for the program, the administration again resorted to moral-*cum*-strategic arguments: by preventing the spread of communism, Point IV would protect world peace and the national security. Administration recommendations for an international information program reflected the same anti-communist bias:

exposing the falsity of communist propaganda would redound to world peace and security for America.

In fact, after 1949 the administration was defending each of its foreign policy proposals as a means of countering a real, but hopefully temporary, communist threat. When he requested congressional approval of U.S. economic aid to South Korea on June 7, 1949, for example, Truman couched his argument solely in the anti-communist terms of the domino theory:

> The survival and progress of the Republic [of South Korea] toward a self-supporting stable economy . . . will encourage the people of southern and southeastern Asia and the islands of the Pacific to resist and reject the communist propaganda with which they are besieged. Moreover, the Korean Republic, by demonstrating the success and tenacity of democracy in resisting communism, will stand as a beacon to the people of northern Asia in resisting the control of the communist forces which have overrun them.

When the House defeated the Korean Aid Bill in early January 1950, Secretary of State Acheson, in a letter to the President, made the "fall" of Korea a threat not only to northern Asia but to international peace. Essentially a political tactic designed to force Congress to reverse itself, the administration released the letter to the press. In part Acheson wrote:

> This action [House defeat of the bill], if not quickly repaired, will have the most far-reaching effects upon our foreign policy, not only in Korea, but in many other areas of the world. . . .
> We are concerned not only about the consequences of this abrupt about-face in Korea, whose government and people have made valiant efforts to win their independence and establish free institutions under the most difficult circumstances, but we are also deeply concerned about the effect which could be created in other parts of the world

where our encouragement is a major element in the struggle for freedom.

Similarly, the themes of American omnipotence and the communist domination—these, rhetorically at least, had by the administration to gain support for its containment policies. Despite the crisis atmosphere in which policy was presented, from 1947 on the administration confidently predicted that adoption of its containment policy was the only way to assure a peaceful postwar world in which American interests would be dominant. Other policy alternatives, they implied, simply did not exist. Opposition to administration policy was disparaged either as unrealistic about Soviet objectives or as a betrayal of the national mission.

Of course, the effectiveness of this argument required popular acceptance of two key administration assumptions: (1) that international change was determined by the decisions of either the United States or the Soviet Union; and (2) that the political success of the United States or the Soviet Union, even in minor areas, would predetermine the character of peace and security in much, if not all, of the world. Both assumptions placed a premium on American response.

The administration's manner of depicting communist weakness also raised unwarranted popular expectations of "liberation." Distinguishing between the peoples of Eastern Europe, China, and the Soviet Union, Truman implied that the people of each country were eager to secure their freedom and looked to the United States to supply it. The Communists remained in power, he said, only by use of terror. At the same time this rhetoric made "liberation" seem a distinct possibility, it heightened popular American fears about internal subversion by implying that a numerically small minority could actually rule a hostile majority. Either way—hope of liberation for the oppressed or subversion of the "free"—this line of administration rhetoric elicited a strong emotional response from the public.

To first contain communist expansion and then to overturn communist domination—these, rhetorically at least, had by 1950 become administration goals. They called for a dual policy of eternal vigilance and superior military strength. Whether championing a large, well-equipped standing army, an improved nuclear technology, an increase in foreign aid— military, technical, or economic—or a greater awareness of the Soviet threat, the administration continually raised both themes. Simultaneously, it sought to represent any negotiations with the Soviet Union as potentially harmful. Negotiations would be desirable, Truman declared, only when the leaders of the Kremlin were convinced that the West would not succumb and when communist societies were reformed along the lines of Western Christian democracy.

BY 1950 this playing off of a crisis atmosphere against a confident optimism about U.S. power had made the American public distinctly anxious. Prodded by administration rhetoric, popular demands for the maximum use of military power against the Russians had increased: America had to *win* over communism. The administration meanwhile sought to undercut every plea for restraint. As much as any other cause, administration rhetoric set the tone of the policy debate over the Korean War.

The North Korean invasion of South Korea created a true political crisis for the Truman administration. It had to enlist popular support for a distant, costly, and seemingly minor conflict and at the same time take care not to provoke the Soviet Union into escalating that conflict into a world war. Since these two objectives were almost diametrically opposed, certain glaring inconsistencies began to appear in administration rhetoric. Thus, while the President on the one hand declared that the "gravity" of the situation required a forthright

American military commitment, on the other hand he counseled a limited use of American military resources. While administration rhetoric might emphasize the importance of the Korean conflict by portraying it in moralistic (Holy Crusade) or strategic (domino theory) terms, administration actions reflected a real appreciation of Soviet interests and the limits to American power.

The continuance of the Korean War heightened popular anxieties that Korea was merely the prelude to future, much larger military confrontations with Russia. Seeking to explain the outbreak of the war in terms of its earlier assurances that containment would ensure an effective peace, the administration only intensified these anxieties. This tack failing, the administration next categorically denied that it had failed to deter aggression. Truman now declared that North Korea's attack confirmed the success of his administration's past policies. The Russians' earlier subversive efforts had indeed been frustrated by American economic aid. Truman explained: "The attack upon Korea makes it plain beyond all doubt that communism has passed beyond the use of subversion to conquer independent nations and will now use armed invasion and war."

America responded in kind. Since, as Truman argued, the North Korean attack amounted to a clear-cut act of aggression, one which posed the threat of a third world war, a forceful demonstration of American power was essential to deter any further Soviet armed moves. To demonstrate America's resolve, the administration instituted a series of far-reaching commitments: it assigned American ground troops to South Korea, strengthened American forces in the Philippines, dispatched the Seventh Fleet to Formosa, and provided military assistance to both the Philippine army and French forces in Indochina. In related moves, the administration sought increased congressional appropriations for the Atomic Energy Commission and military aid to Greece,

Turkey, and Iran. It also pressed for congressional approval of a military-aid program to establish a well-equipped standing army in Western Europe; this program included West German rearmament and the deployment of American troops in Europe. As evidenced by a December 1, 1950, presidential request for additional defense appropriations from Congress, all these military movements and appropriations requests were made in crisis-laden, moralistic terms.

> The gravity of the world şituation requires that these funds be made available with the utmost speed.
> . . . These funds are needed to support our part in the United Nations military action in Korea, and to increase the size and readiness of our armed forces should action become necessary in other parts of the world.
> . . . The further expansion of our military forces and of our atomic energy enterprise are directed toward strengthening the defenses of the United States and of the entire free world. This expansion is a matter of great urgency, which can be understood and evaluated against the background of present critical world conditions.
> United States troops . . . are fighting for freedom and against tyranny—for law and order and against brutal aggression. The attack of the North Korean communists . . . , if unchecked, would have blasted all hope of a just and lasting peace—for if open aggression had been unopposed in Korea, it would have been an invitation to aggression elsewhere.

In 1951 and 1952 the administration expressed this same sense of alarm when justifying the economic and military sacrifices that would be necessary for its Korean policy. Specifically, it argued that only superior military strength could bring about peace and that the North Korean attack was not indigenous—was, in fact, Soviet-directed. Playing on popular fears, Truman exclaimed: "Our homes, our Nation, all the things we believe in, are in great danger." "We are fighting for freedom," he said, "for the right to worship as we please, in any church that we choose to attend, [for] the right to read what we please, and the right to elect public officials of our own choosing." Truman raised these same fears in justifying the assignment of U.S. troops to Europe because of "the worldwide menace of Communist imperialism," and the necessity for greater civil defense appropriations because "I cannot tell you when or where the attack will come or that it will come at all. I can only remind you that we must be ready when it does come."

Initially, the administration abjurred any limits on the American military response in Korea. At late 1950 press conferences, Truman refused to disavow the possibility of America's use of nuclear weapons in Korea or to specifically restrict American troops to the Korean peninsula. His reaction to the disclosure of Chinese Communist troops in Korea was identical: he would not deny that U.S. troops might be sent to the Chinese mainland or that nuclear weapons might be used there. Because of national security, he argued, the United States could not in conscience or with reason refrain from responding vigorously to Chinese involvement in the war. Almost as an aside, Truman maintained that the noble defensive motives of the Americans as opposed to the alien expansionism of the communists insured a U.S. victory in Korea. His November 30, 1950, presidential statement on Chinese Communist intervention emphasized these points:

> Recent developments in Korea confront the world with a serious crisis. The Chinese Communist leaders have sent their troops from Manchuria to launch a strong and well-organized attack against the United Nations forces in North Korea.
>
> If the United Nations yields to the forces of aggression, no nation will be safe or secure. If aggression is successful in Korea, we can expect it to spread throughout Asia and Europe to this hemisphere. We are fighting in Korea for our own national security and survival. . . . We hope that the Chinese people will not continue to be forced or deceived into serving the ends of Russian colonial policy in Asia.

By 1951 Truman's hotted-up rhetoric had caused a loss of credibility in his administration. On the one hand, the administration repeatedly emphasized the gravity of the crisis posed by Soviet subversion and expansionism and expressed confidence in eventual success if the American public only possessed the necessary will and purpose to carry out Truman's policies. All the while it continued to characterize the U.S.-Soviet opposition as a confrontation between American Christian selflessness and communist atheistic expansionism. On the other hand, quite apart from the forcefulness of its rhetoric, the administration was actually pursuing a policy of restraint in its use of military power, conducting its military operations within firm strategic guidelines. In point of fact, American military potential, particularly nuclear weapons, was by no means fully utilized in Korea: the air war was limited to the Korean peninsula, and Chinese Nationalist troops were confined to Formosa. Nor did the administration use either potential military resources or diplomatic pressure to effect the liberation of the "satellite" peoples. The Chinese Nationalists were prevented from attempting to free the mainland Chinese; Eastern European exiles were neither encouraged nor supplied with weapons; and, despite Soviet violations, the administration opposed congressional efforts to repudiate the Yalta agreements.

These military and political restrictions were inconsistent with the total war against communism which the administration advertised in its rhetoric, and they were in direct contradiction to its projection of what would come about if Soviet subversion were not vigorously confronted. Indeed, if the Soviet threat was world-wide, if world peace and the very liberties of the American people were ultimately threatened by the Korean conflict—and the Truman administration had repeatedly said as much—then nothing less than the full use of American military might in Korea was required. Thus, to countenance military and political restraint, as Truman and his administration clearly did, seemed to be either a misunderstanding of the seriousness of the communist threat to American security or a dereliction of duty. To argue that restraint was necessary to prevent the escalation of Korea into a world war seemed to reflect a staggering ignorance of the Soviet Union's basic intention—as Truman had time and again declared it to be—of utterly destroying Western Christian democracy.

The inconsistencies between the Truman administration's go-for-broke rhetoric and its cautious military response in Korea paved the way for the success of Joseph McCarthy and his followers. The moralistic and defensive tenor of administration rhetoric, its stress on the American "mission," its emphasis on national security, and its strained definition of communist subversion—all served to create a climate in which such terms as "sell-out," "betrayal," "liberation," and "victory," could be successfully used by the McCarthyites against the Truman administration. By exploiting the inconsistencies between administration rhetoric and response, McCarthy and other congressional conservatives were able to "explain" that the real Soviet threat to the national security was internal subversion. They thereby capitalized on both fears of a third world war and doubts about the administration's methods and intentions in foreign affairs.

The McCarthyites never did, nor were they required to, formulate an alternative course to Truman's. Instead, because of the inconsistency between administration rhetoric and response, they were able to concentrate on criticizing past administration policy decisions and personnel. Because the administration had set an American peace as its rhetorical goal, the McCarthyites could blame the "failure" to achieve that peace on either the administration's ignorance of the threat of communism, or its lax security procedures which enabled communists and their sympathizers to infiltrate the government and help bring about pro-Soviet policies. Although this critique was simplistic, conspiratorial at its base, and rather sleazily moralistic, it nonetheless neatly used administration rhetoric to condemn administration policy. Through its own rhetoric, the Truman administration had closed the vicious circle on itself. All the McCarthyites had to do was chase around it.

4

Sell-out and Betrayal: The Yalta Episode

PERIODICALLY DURING the late 1940's and early 1950's, congressional conservatives pointed to the Yalta agreements—especially the secrecy surrounding them and their provisions about Eastern Europe and the Far East—as confirmation that the Roosevelt administration's policy at Yalta had contributed to, if it did not create, the Soviet threat to American national security. Although directed at specific policy decisions, this criticism also focused on the membership of the U.S. Yalta delegation. The McCarthyites' main contention was that the sinister and secretive character of the Yalta agreements, so contrary to American interests and traditions, indicated that communists, or at a minimum pro-communists, had taken part on the administration's side in the negotiations. In short, they charged that the threat to national security stemmed from communist infiltration of the Roosevelt and Truman administrations; that the problem was therefore one not simply of error or mistaken judgment but of treason and betrayal; and that new leadership, untainted by communist leanings or sympathies, was the only hope to remove this subversive threat and bring about victory in the Cold War.

Popular belief in the subversive character of the Yalta Conference derived directly from the agreements concluded there.

The first were the Eastern European agreements establishing Poland's postwar borders and, until free elections could be held, administrative procedures (occupation policy and the selection of provisional governments) for the liberated areas. The second were the German agreements on occupation zones and reparations payments. The last, and ultimately the most controversial, were the Far Eastern agreements which ceded to the Soviet Union "pre-eminent" rights to the use of Port Arthur and Dairen, joint ownership of the Manchurian railroad, and control of South Sakhalin and the Kurile islands. The Soviet Union was granted these concessions in return for its promise to enter the war against Japan three months after the end of the war in Europe and to conclude a treaty of alliance with the Chinese Nationalist government.

Behind the criticisms of Yalta were the spirit and character of Roosevelt's diplomacy at the conference: his willingness to negotiate in good faith with the Soviet Union and his implicit belief that Soviet promises could be trusted; the secrecy of the conference proceedings and certain of its agreements; and FDR's failure to consult or fully inform Congress and the public about policy objectives and decisions either before or after the conference. All this ran counter to the later Cold War spirit, as did the Roosevelt administration's security procedures at the conference. In one instance, disdain for the loyalty screening techniques championed by the FBI and conservative Congressmen had led to Alger Hiss's attendance at Yalta as an adviser to Secretary of State Edward Stettinius.

In fact, none of Roosevelt's policy at Yalta was in line with later Cold War norms. Through compromise and concession Roosevelt had sought to reach accommodation with the Soviet Union. Recognizing the extent of Soviet power and the strategy of her geographic position, he had conceded the inevitability of Soviet influence in Eastern Europe and North China, trying meanwhile to avert Soviet domination of those areas by a diplomacy based on limited concessions and mutual understanding. The tripartite Allied commission for supervision of Eastern Europe (conceding a Soviet veto on consultations) and the Far Eastern provisions (conceding a Soviet presence in North China and Manchuria) reflected this recognition of the inevitability of a postwar Soviet role in both areas. Since Roosevelt had implicitly assumed that Soviet objectives were limited and legitimate, his concessions represented an attempt to minimize intervention and confrontation.

But both policy and attitude changed with the Truman administration. The rationale behind Yalta—that a negotiated agreement with the Soviet Union was possible and that the development of mutual trust was the best means to a just and lasting peace—was now rejected in favor of the containment policy and superior military strength. As the loyalty of federal employees became a basic governmental concern—the existence of even one disloyal employee constituting a "serious" threat to national security—the security procedures before, and especially Hiss's presence at, Yalta created doubts about the delegation's character and raised suspicions about the "real" factors for administration secrecy—Roosevelt's in 1945 and Truman's thereafter. In addition, the postwar communization of Eastern Europe and China seemed to demonstrate the hollowness of the democratic, internationalist provisions of the Yalta agreements; in fact, many critics now felt the Yalta agreements had made that communization possible in the first place.

The Truman administration's own post-Yalta policy contributed to these popular assumptions by encouraging a critical view of the conference. The adoption of the containment policy, the continual recitation of American omnipotence, and the regular rejection of summit diplomacy all served to discredit the diplomacy of Yalta. In the context of the administration's representation of the Cold War as a confrontation between good and evil, Yalta emerged as an immoral compromise and a distinct betrayal of American ideals. Once again, it seemed, American diplomats had been duped. By augmenting Soviet power, the Yalta Conference had made a third world war possible.

This change in national priorities enabled McCarthy and his supporters to use the Yalta agreements to flail the policies and personnel of the Roosevelt administration. And Truman's defense of the conference and the continuity of State Department personnel enabled McCarthyites to indict his administration as well. The thrust of their critique was that Yalta should not have occurred to begin with, and must under no circumstances be repeated. A more dynamic and forthright policy, it followed, required the immediate repudiation of the Yalta agreements and "Yalta men."

While the change in national priorities made the Yalta Conference a symbol of "lost peace" and "treason and betrayal," the McCarthyite attack got its greatest mileage from the controversial Far Eastern aspects of the agreements. Not disclosed in the original February 11, 1945, conference communiqué, these agreements had been controversial since their release exactly one year later. Initially, criticism centered on the delay in publication, but in time the agreements and concessions themselves came under attack. This attack, which had far-reaching domestic political consequences, came as a direct result of Communist China's defeat of the Nationalists and its subsequent intervention in the Korean War.

The sudden collapse of the Nationalist cause in 1948–1949 caught most Americans by surprise. Convinced by the Truman administration and the American press of Chiang Kai-shek's popularity and the alien character of communism to the Chinese, the public found the Nationalists' defeat inconceivable. Its reaction to the communization of China, however, did not lead to a reassessment of either Chiang or communism, but to the belief that the takeover had been engineered by Moscow.*

The intensification of the Cold War and the rhetoric of the Truman administration had helped to shape the popular view that revolutionary change in China was essentially a cover for Soviet subversion. The size of China and her potentially valuable economic resources added to the belief that the defeat of Chiang represented an American setback and a Soviet victory.

By 1950 these assumptions provided the basis for a searching criticism of the Truman administration's priorities and personnel. It had by this time come to seem that administration policy, and not Chiang's leadership, had contributed most to the Communist success.† This belief also permitted

---

* In a December 1948 poll, 51 per cent thought that the Chinese Communists took orders from Moscow, 10 per cent did not, while 18 per cent had no opinion. Questioned whether the United States should aid Nationalist China, 28 per cent favored, 4 per cent favored with qualifications, 34 per cent opposed, and 13 per cent had no opinion. Asked whether military aid (not troops) should be provided, 39 per cent approved, 23 per cent disapproved, and 10 per cent had no opinion. A sharp change of opinion came about in May 1949, when 43 per cent supported noninvolvement in the Chinese civil war, 4 per cent thought the war was a lost cause, 27 per cent supported military or economic aid, and 14 per cent claimed no opinion. In September of the same year, when asked what the United States should do to prevent China from going communist, 45 per cent didn't know, 36 per cent favored no aid, while 2 per cent favored aid in the form of propaganda, 4 per cent economic aid, 7 per cent military aid, and 8 per cent general aid. Most Americans simply did not support involvement in the Chinese civil war or see any viable options to involvement.

† In fact, since 1945 the Truman administration had actively aided Chiang while publicly professing neutrality in the Chinese civil war. When formulating the Truman Doctrine and Marshall Plan, however, the administration had intentionally confined the scope of its aid proposals to Europe. In part, this limitation derived from European-centrism; in part, from the political necessity of avoiding an image of world-wide commitments and limitless expenditures, whether political, military, or economic.

moderate Republicans to join in the attack on Yalta and the administration's China policy. Although moderates and conservatives continued to differ about bipartisanship and internationalism—moderates being for them, conservatives against—the moderates were able to deny that their criticisms of the Yalta Far Eastern agreements harmed bipartisanship since no Republican had been consulted about or participated in those agreements. At the same time, they could assert that, in contrast to European policy, the administration's China policy had failed because the containment approach had not been adopted. While sustaining their critique of bipartisanship and internationalism, the conservatives on the other hand were free to assail the administration for what they felt to be its policies of appeasement and unilateralism which brought about the Nationalists' defeat.

This criticism of Yalta occurred in the context of the crisis-in-confidence that started with the outbreak of the Korean War in June 1950 and continued through the intervention of the Chinese Communists in Korea in December 1950. The administration's assertion, an assertion made repeatedly since 1947, that the United States could determine the character of the postwar world, now seemed dubious in the extreme. Why had the Korean War occurred? Why were the Chinese not deterred from interceding in the war? Why was the administration not fully using American power to speedily resolve the war?

Combined with mistrust of past administration propaganda, these doubts made it seem that the Korean stalemate, if not the whole Cold War, was the clear result of the Truman administration's reluctance to confront communism. Thus the McCarthyites blamed earlier administration actions— removal of U.S. troops from Korea in 1949, Acheson's temporizing statement in 1950 about the U.S. "defense perimeter," and, most importantly, the August 1945 U.S.-Soviet occupation agreement that divided Korea at the 38th parallel—for providing the opportunity for communist expansion that led to the war.

While Korea itself remained uppermost in the public mind, McCarthyites moved on to the Chinese Communist intervention, using it as the basis for a searching reassessment of the administration's past China policy. First they blamed Chiang Kai-shek's defeat on the Yalta agreements which had ceded Chinese ports and control of the Manchurian railroad to the Soviet Union and which allowed Soviet troops to occupy Manchuria. Then, noting the limited Soviet military role in the war against Japan (the Russians entered it a mere six days before the Japanese surrender) and America's successful development of the atomic bomb, the congressional conservatives questioned whether Soviet military aid had been needed at all in 1945. Had the United States been able to do without the Soviets then—and the McCarthyites claimed she could—then the Yalta agreements with their concessions to the Soviet Union need never have been made. Thus, the McCarthyites claimed, administration negotiation at Yalta, far from being in any way helpful, had only brought about the Korean War and the Communist Chinese intervention in that war.*

Past administration errors of judgment and indeed of loyalty became a major McCarthyite charge. In fact, the McCarthyites devised a sequence of error which began with the administration's refusal during the 1940's to give the Nationalists and South Koreans adequate military and diplomatic aid, continued at Yalta and in General Marshall's mission to China in 1945–1946, and culminated in the collapse of Chiang and the Communist victory. This chain of error, McCarthyites charged, would continue to compound

* As in the popular assessment of the Chinese Communist victory over the Nationalists, most Americans believed that Chinese intervention in the Korean War had been directed by Moscow. In one poll, 81 per cent held this view.

itself so long as the same men formulated policy. In support of this contention, they cited the administration's refusal during the Korean War to use nuclear weapons, to lend the Chinese Nationalists military support, or to extend American conventional bombing across the Yalu River. When General MacArthur was recalled from Korea by Truman, the McCarthyites' dossier was complete.

This same attack on past administration policy and personnel constituted the McCarthyites' entire strategy during Senate hearings on MacArthur's dismissal. That strategy had two purposes: (1) to divert attention from the actual reasons why Truman had dismissed MacArthur (the McCarthyites wished to avoid a debate over civil-military relations); and (2) to document administration errors that had contributed to the Korean War and the China debacle, thereby indirectly confirming MacArthur's consistently correct, and the administration's consistently wrong, assessment of Far Eastern politics. In fulfilling this second purpose, the McCarthyites brought out all their charges about Russian involvement in the Far East. Questioning the rationale for the Yalta Far Eastern concessions, concluded by Roosevelt but defended by Truman, and Alger Hiss's presence at the conference, they concluded that both confirmed the existence of a serious internal-security threat. In fact, they charged, the Truman administration was "soft toward communism."

The administration's initial failure to publish the Far Eastern agreements made at Yalta gave added weight to the McCarthyites' charges of subversion and betrayal. The Roosevelt and Truman administrations, they claimed, had not published the agreements because they had not wanted the public to know what they were doing. It was as simple as that. In addition, earlier, in March 1945, the Roosevelt administration's assurances that the major Yalta agreements had already been released would raise popular suspicions that still other secret agreements remained undisclosed.

The truth was that, although formally committed to fulfilling the promises made at Yalta, the Truman administration had in 1945 sought to preclude enactment of the Far Eastern agreements by not publishing them. This double-edged policy of formally adhering to the Yalta agreements while covertly being opposed to them derived from the administration's desire to maximize its international options. In 1945 the confrontation between the U.S. and Russia centered on Eastern Europe, Germany, atomic arms control, and the United Nations. Since the administration based its position in this confrontation on Soviet failure to adhere to the Yalta terms, it felt it could not very well publish additional agreements—i.e., the Far Eastern ones—which it had no intention of fulfilling. What was more, the Far East was not then an important issue: certain liberals and radicals excepted, the administration's protestations of its neutrality in the Chinese civil war were still accepted at face value. Thus, to have published the agreements in 1945 would have been to raise, both at home and in the Kremlin, questions about administration policy the answers to which the administration was not yet prepared to give. Unfortunately for the administration, this delaying tactic backfired: whereas the agreements would probably have won popular support in 1945, their coming to light in 1946 only served to arouse popular fears about further "secret" agreements.

HISTORICALLY, American policy toward China had been based essentially on the self-righteous view that the Open Door policy had promoted Chinese independence. According to this view, the only objective of the Open Door had been to promote the evolution of a united, democratic China free from European and Japanese intervention. In truth, the policy had been neither so noble nor so altruistic as the public still liked to believe, though it did conform to contemporary American anti-colonial feeling.

World War II added a new dimension to America's paternalistic interest in China. In one sense, Roosevelt considered a strong China a counterweight to the resurgence of an expansionistic Japan while concurrently reducing British and Russian influence in the Far East. In another sense, he hoped that a democratic China would serve as a symbol for other Asian peoples fighting European colonialism and Soviet communism. Because most Americans either shared these views or were too concerned about achieving an Allied military victory to contradict him, Roosevelt did not have to expend much energy shaping public opinion on China. This left him free to pursue his primary Far Eastern objective: the creation of a democracy in China. To succeed, this objective rested on two conditions: (1) the defeat and demilitarization of Japan and, along with it, the liberation of China from Japanese occupation; and (2) a resolution of the Chinese civil war that precluded British or Soviet attempts to extend their influence in the country.

Yet meeting these two conditions posed seemingly insurmountable problems. In the first place, the British, who were committed to maintaining their imperial position, had both economic and strategic interests in the Far East. Secondly, owing partly to the deployment of American troops on both the Atlantic and Pacific fronts, partly to the Soviet Union's geographic position and large troop strength, the defeat of Japan seemed to require Soviet military help. The Russians, so Roosevelt reasoned, could expedite not only the defeat of Japan but the liberation of China—the latter, hopefully, while avoiding the danger of the Chinese Communists liberating North China from the Japanese. On the other hand, Soviet involvement would necessarily increase Soviet postwar influence in the Far East and possibly frustrate the administration's political objectives of resolving the

Chinese civil war by establishing a Chinese democracy. Thus realism called for Soviet intervention, but prudence dictated that postwar Soviet involvement, both military and political, be very strictly defined and limited. As such, Roosevelt's policy during World War II was based on the dual—and, as many would later see it, contradictory—objectives of maximizing Soviet military aid while minimizing Soviet postwar influence.

By the time Yalta convened, the Soviet entrance into the Far Eastern war was no longer' an issue but a fact: it had been agreed to at Teheran in 1943 and reaffirmed in 1944 during discussions between Stalin and U.S. Ambassador Averell Harriman. Thus the principal issue at Yalta was merely the timing of that entrance and its inevitable postwar implications. In return for a Soviet commitment to enter the Far Eastern war three months after the end of the war in Europe, Roosevelt made certain territorial or political concessions, among them lease rights to the Chinese ports of Dairen and Port Arthur, joint Soviet and Chinese control of the Chinese East Manchurian Railroad, and Soviet control of the Japanese territories of South Sakhalin and the Kuriles. The one qualification to these concessions was that the port and railroad provisions, because they affected the interests of a wartime ally, China, would have to be ratified by a treaty between the Soviet Union and China before becoming operative. Such a treaty, one of mutual friendship and security, would obviously imply Soviet recognition of the Chinese Nationalist government and the disavowal of any aid or support to the Chinese Communists. President Roosevelt agreed to use his administration's good offices to secure Chiang's assent to these concessions. He further promised Stalin not to inform Chiang about the Far Eastern agreements until after the conclusion of the war in Europe. This arrangement was based on purely wartime considerations. Both Roosevelt and Stalin wished to avert a Japanese assault on Siberia, which would have required diverting Soviet troops from Europe before the war there was over.

§●

THE VAGUE WORDING of the Yalta Far Eastern agreements presented formidable unresolved diplomatic problems for the Truman administration when it assumed power in April 1945. On the surface, the concessions did not seem major. In fact, however, the Yalta agreements did not clearly define the extent of the postwar Soviet role in either China or Japan. Although certain agreements had already been concluded, Truman still felt he had two options left in April. First, he had to decide whether the United States should remain committed to Soviet involvement in the Far East. If he decided affirmatively, he then had to determine what role to cede to the Russians in the matter of the occupation of Japan, and how strictly to interpret the Yalta concessions regarding China. In connection with this latter question was the extent to which the United States ought to support, militarily and diplomatically, the Chinese Nationalists during Sino-Soviet discussions on the Yalta agreements.

As soon as he became President, Truman was beset by pressure from hard-liners in the State Department, the Foreign Service, and his own Cabinet to revise or revoke the Yalta commitments. A few days after Roosevelt's death, at a briefing on foreign policy, Truman received conflicting interpretations of the Soviet Union's Far Eastern objectives. On the one hand, U.S. Ambassador to China Patrick Hurley optimistically affirmed the Soviet Union's willingness to refrain from intervention in the Nationalist-Communist conflict; the Soviets were committed, he said, to a united, democratic China. On the other hand, U.S. Ambassador to the Soviet Union W. Averell Harriman and George Kennan, the U.S. chargé d'affaires in Moscow, expressed distrust and suspicion of Russia's China policy, and cautioned against undue reliance on Soviet good faith.

These conflicting views were the basis for an April 23 Cabinet meeting at which the U.S. position on the Far Eastern agreements was reappraised. Distressed over Soviet actions in Eastern Europe, Truman suggested that the failure of any Yalta signatory to fulfill any of its commitments might free the other signatories from fulfilling theirs. In so doing, Truman was anticipating a Soviet rejection of administration protests over Eastern Europe, which, according to his proposed interpretation of the Yalta agreements, would enable the United States to renounce its Far Eastern concessions. The main opposition to this position came from the military. Summing up the counter-argument, General George Marshall, then chairman of the Joint Chiefs of Staff, maintained that the Far Eastern war could not be won without Soviet military assistance. In his estimate, the concessions had to stand.

While no formal Cabinet decision on the concessions was reached in April 1945, the German surrender on May 8 led to a further administration re-evaluation of Yalta. On May 12 Acting Secretary of State Joseph C. Grew sent memoranda to Secretary of War Stimson and Secretary of the Navy Forrestal asking that the military services state their views on the Far Eastern agreements. The memoranda also detailed the State Department's objections to the Yalta concessions as well as its suspicions of Soviet aims. The question posed was: Should the United States remain committed to enactment of the Yalta terms, and, if so, in whole or in part? In a May 21 reply from Stimson, the War Department again emphasized the importance of Soviet military assistance to the early defeat of Japan. Stimson went on to say that Soviet influence in the Far East was inevitable, and that a Big Three conference to discuss and possibly revise the Yalta concessions would be undesirable. Thus, while the War Department remained suspicious of Soviet objectives and committed to a policy of limiting Soviet influence, Stimson still believed that the administration could not successfully renegotiate the terms set at Yalta and, further, argued that the effort to do so could only delay the timing of Soviet military intervention without reducing postwar Soviet influence in the area.

Despite these tactical differences between the State and War Departments, administration policy shifted dramatically by May. Not formally opposed to the Yalta concessions, the Truman administration pursued a policy of cooperation with Russia. This policy, however, was geared not to appeasement but to the attainment of certain major United States objectives: a definite Soviet commitment to the Chinese Nationalist government, a limitation of Soviet territorial demands on China, and a pledge against Soviet aid or encouragement to the Chinese Communists.*

Yet the administration's actions in April and May—among them the abrupt cut-off of lend-lease; the sharp, uncompromising, and self-righteous tone of Truman's meeting with Soviet Foreign Minister Molotov; and United States reluctance to develop a coordinated policy toward the strategic areas of Eastern Europe, the Mediterranean, Latin America, and China—could not have facilitated its winning Soviet cooperation on China. To repair damages and allay Stalin's suspicions about the new administration, on May 23 Truman dispatched Harry Hopkins to Moscow. Because of his long

---

* As for Japan, in the various discussions at the London (September 1945) and Moscow (December 1945) Foreign Ministers meetings, and in direct discussions between U.S. Ambassador Harriman and Premier Stalin during the summer and fall of 1945, the United States sought to limit Soviet influence in postwar Japan by insuring U.S. control of occupation policy. While the Russians were not formally excluded from a role in occupied Japan, basic policy decisions were to be made only by the U.S. commander, General Douglas MacArthur. The Allied control commission was to ratify decisions and provide general guidelines. The objective of this diplomacy was to avert a duplication of the joint occupation of Germany.

association with the Roosevelt administration and his friendly personal relations with Stalin, Hopkins was an ideal emissary.

While the Hopkins mission succeeded somewhat in mitigating Stalin's suspicions about Truman, it also forced the issue of the Yalta Far Eastern agreements. On May 28 Stalin reaffirmed his government's intention, which he had pledged at Yalta, to enter the Far Eastern war. He also told Hopkins that the time was right to initiate discussions between the Soviet Union and the Chinese Nationalists on the Yalta concessions to Russia. The Soviet Union, Stalin stipulated, would be ready to enter the war against Japan on August 8, but only on the condition that a Sino-Soviet treaty had been successfully concluded by then.

In response to the Hopkins mission, at least on the formal policy level, the Truman administration could now only reaffirm its commitment to Soviet involvement in the Far Eastern war and the implementation of the Yalta terms. Privately, however, the administration retained its reservations about those terms as well as its suspicions about Soviet objectives and good faith. Thus Truman continued to try either to avert Soviet involvement or, failing that, to insure that the Far Eastern agreements would not provide an opening for Soviet influence in Japan, North China, or Manchuria.

The Hopkins mission also meant that the administration could delay Sino-Soviet discussions no longer. On June 9 Truman personally informed Chinese Foreign Minister T. V. Soong of the Yalta provisions concerning China and urged Soong to initiate negotiations with the Soviet Union. U.S. Ambassador to China Patrick Hurley was also instructed to inform Chinese Premier Chiang Kai-shek of the Yalta terms.

In a June 14 meeting with Soong, Truman reported the substance of Hopkins' May 28 conversations with Stalin, particularly the Premier's affirmation of support for the Nationalist government and his statement that no leader but

Chiang could insure unity in China. Still concerned about the ramifications of the Yalta concessions for his country and the weakness of the Chinese negotiating position *vis-à-vis* the Soviet Union, Soong sought to establish a definite United States commitment to China. First, he pressed for a United States pledge to co-sign, and thereby accept the obligation to act upon, any treaty concluded between China and the Soviet Union. Second, he suggested that the status of Port Arthur be guaranteed by the Four Powers. Third, he asked Truman to define the U.S. interpretation of that section of the Yalta agreements which ceded "pre-eminent interest" to the Soviet Union in the areas surrounding Port Arthur and Dairen. Truman refused to consider any of these requests. Thus, as he left Washington for Moscow, Soong had no firm understanding of the extent of U.S. support for China during the Moscow negotiations.

꿍

THE ADMINISTRATION'S POSITION during the Soong talks had been to inform the Chinese of the Yalta terms and suggest that discussions be initiated—and no more. Subsequently, in both the first phase of the talks (June 30 through July 14) and the final stage preparatory to the conclusion of a formal treaty (August 7 through August 14), the administration assumed an ambivalent stance, never formally opposing or denouncing Soviet demands and always refusing to clarify the United States position with regard to the Chinese.

This noncommittal position on the part of the U.S. deeply troubled the Chinese throughout their difficult discussions with the Soviets. With the inception of the formal talks on June 30, Stalin stipulated as the Soviet condition for a pact of friendship the resolution of outstanding Sino-Soviet differences deriving from the Yalta terms. This included Chinese acceptance of the independence of Outer Mongolia, the

Soviet right to administer the Manchurian railroad jointly with the Chinese, and Soviet "lease" rights to and "pre-eminent interest" in Dairen and Port Arthur. In the ensuing negotiations, Stalin adopted an even harder position than he had taken at Yalta, attempting by an extension of the Yalta concessions to assure a dominant Soviet role in Manchuria and to secure what amounted to a Soviet sphere of influence in the Kuantung peninsula.

During the June 30–July 14 meetings the status of Outer Mongolia was amicably resolved. But Soong and Stalin continued to differ over Soviet rights in Dairen and Port Arthur. Seeking U.S. support for his efforts to limit Soviet demands, Soong pressed Ambassador Harriman for a clarification of the United States interpretation of these rights. Harriman in turn requested advice from the Truman administration; on July 4 the administration reiterated its refusal to be bound by any specific interpretation of the Yalta terms. Its position was that clarification would indirectly involve the United States in the negotiations and hence implicitly bind it to fulfilling the settlement that resulted. While the administration was eager to sustain its independence of the Moscow negotiations, it nevertheless did not wish to disavow interest; thus, on July 6, Secretary of State Byrnes instructed Harriman to inform the Russians that, as a signatory to the Yalta agreements, the United States must be consulted *before* the final approval of a Sino-Soviet treaty.

Still pressured by Soong about America's seeming indifference to the fate of China, on July 9 Harriman again urged the administration to report its understanding of the Yalta terms, this time directly to Stalin. Concurrent with this request, the State Department had in fact drafted a memorandum urging United States support of China at the Moscow negotiations. Outlining the Department's interpretation of the Yalta concessions, this memorandum stressed the need to restrict Soviet influence. It pointed out that acceptance of the

Soviet proposals concerning the railroads and Dairen "would represent a reversion to a situation which was one of the most pernicious foci of imperialism." Accordingly, it recommended that the United States attempt to influence the Soviet government to modify its demands toward China. Nonetheless, the administration made no formal decision either on the State Department's recommendation or on Harriman's request. While Harriman kept in informal contact with Soong, encouraging him to stand firm but offering no specific advice or commitment, the Sino-Soviet talks finally reached a stalemate. After stressing his inability to accede to Stalin's demands on port rights, Soong broke off the negotiations on July 14 and returned to Chunking for further consultations with Chiang Kai-shek.

§♠

WHILE THE United States attitude throughout this preliminary negotiating period had seemed ambivalent, its ambivalence was indicative not of administration indifference—as Soong felt—but of the desire to forestall Soviet influence in the Far East as long as possible. Since the Soviet Union had declared its unwillingness to enter the war against Japan *until* a treaty had been concluded with China, by delaying negotiations on that treaty the administration hoped to avert the inevitable extension of Soviet influence through successful American military operations without repudiating the terms laid down at Yalta.

By June the administration options had increased as the result of the defeat of Germany and U.S. progress on the development of the atomic bomb. Thereafter the administration operated on the premise, one wholly contrary to the spirit in which Roosevelt's Yalta policy was made, that Soviet military involvement against Japan was not imperative. This shift was revealed on June 18 in a formal change of position by the

Joint Chiefs of Staff. While continuing to emphasize the importance of Soviet military aid to the defeat of Japan and the liberation of China, the Joint Chiefs now described that aid as desirable but not indispensable. Specifically, they recommended that the United States *not* bargain for Soviet involvement.

With all this in mind, President Truman and Secretary of State Byrnes discussed the Far East with Premier Stalin and Foreign Minister Molotov at the Potsdam Conference on July 17. First the Soviet leaders informed Truman and Byrnes of their willingness to accept Chinese control of Manchuria as well as to recognize the Nationalists as the sole leaders of China. In reply, Byrnes affirmed that the United States held to a strict interpretation of the Yalta terms. Then, feigning ignorance of the recently concluded Soong-Stalin talks, he expressed United States concern over their progress. Byrnes sounded Stalin out about the grounds for Sino-Soviet disagreement. On the basis of Stalin's reply, Byrnes and Truman concluded that the differences between the Soviet and Chinese positions were so fundamental that, at least in the immediate future, a Sino-Soviet treaty was highly unlikely. (This conclusion also underlay Winston Churchill's assessment of the United States position. Following a July 23 meeting with Byrnes, Churchill decided that the United States no longer wanted Soviet assistance in the war against Japan.)

The Potsdam discussions between the U.S. and Soviet military staffs provided further assurances for the administration that the Russians still demanded a Sino-Soviet treaty as a necessary precondition for entering the Japanese war. At a July 24 meeting between the two military staffs, General Antonov, the Soviet commander on the Far Eastern front, informed the U.S. delegation that Soviet troops were massed for an attack and would be prepared to launch an offensive in the latter half of August. But Antonov emphasized that the exact date of the offensive would depend upon the satisfactory conclusion of negotiations with the Chinese Nationalists.

Although at Potsdam the administration had been primarily involved in discussions about Eastern Europe and Germany, it had also remained in contact with the Chinese Nationalists. On July 20 Chiang Kai-shek informed Truman about Soong's mission. (Truman had already been fully briefed about it by Harriman.) Since the Chinese had bargained in good faith, Chiang argued, they could make no further concessions to secure the treaty. What was he now to do? Truman agreed that no more concessions be made—in fact he directed Chiang specifically *not* to make them. Yet, despite this, he continued to insist then that the Yalta terms be carried out. He then urged Chiang to have Soong return to Moscow to continue negotiations. (On July 28 Byrnes instructed Soong through Ambassador Hurley to ask Stalin to resume discussions on unresolved issues on July 30 or 31.)

While the administration continued formally to support the Yalta commitments, in view of the July 17 meeting with Stalin and Molotov, its instructions to Chiang—if Soong adhered to them—would effectively stymie the conclusion of the treaty. Moreover, by July the successful development of the atomic bomb had reduced the need for Soviet help in the Japanese war. Finally, recent differences with the Soviets over occupation policy in Eastern Europe had led to a more rigid U.S. bargaining position. Instead of consulting the Soviets, the administration abruptly acted unilaterally by drafting a formal declaration demanding unconditional Japanese surrender; it had also decided to accept the Japanese request of August 10 for clarification of the surrender terms. By not consulting the Soviet leaders on these matters, the administration further minimized the importance of the Soviet role in the war against Japan.

Once the second phase of the Sino-Soviet discussions began, the United States adopted a rigid stance, advising the

Chinese to stand firm even if that firmness prevented agreement. On August 5 Byrnes asked Harriman officially to inform Soong that the United States opposed concessions beyond those agreed to at Yalta. He warned the Chinese specifically not to make further concessions over the status of Dairen or Soviet reparation and "war booty" demands. In contrast to its earlier silence, the essence of the administration's new position was to support the Chinese at the same time it opposed the conclusion of the treaty; only if the Soviet Union reversed her attitude and radically changed her demands would the administration relent. At almost any cost, it did not wish to repeat in the Far East what had happened in Europe as a result of excessive Soviet influence.

ON ONE LEVEL, this policy of the Truman administration failed, for it did not in fact forestall the Soviet Union's entrance into the Japanese war. Although a formal Sino-Soviet treaty had not been concluded, and although the United States finally had neither requested nor encouraged Soviet intervention, the Russians nonetheless declared war on Japan on August 8 (two days after Hiroshima) and moved their troops into North China and Manchuria. Simultaneous with this invasion, Stalin warned Soong on August 10 that, should a formal Sino-Soviet agreement not be concluded, Chinese Communist troops would be permitted to move into Manchuria. Fearful of Soviet support of the Chinese Communists, Chiang Kai-shek acceded to the Soviet demands on the unresolved issues. The formal Sino-Soviet treaty was now quickly concluded, its terms announced on August 14 (which was also the date of the Japanese surrender). Thus the administration's dual strategy of postponement and inflexibility had left the Nationalists in the lurch, completely vulnerable to Soviet intervention. An excess of cunning had led the administration to ignore political-military realities. Although the manner differed greatly from the McCarthyites' later charges, it was indeed the Truman administration's shortsightedness that had in essence "betrayed" the Nationalists.

Similarly, the administration's indirect opposition to the Yalta provisions created the potential for U.S.-Soviet division once the war with Japan ended. The rapidity of the Japanese surrender and the last-minute Soviet entry into the war complicated surrender proceedings. The administration had had little time to devise formal terms delineating to whom Japanese troops should surrender. It thus directed Japanese troops to surrender to the Nationalists in all areas of China south of Manchuria and to the Russians in Manchuria, Korea north of the 38th parallel, and Karafutu. These surrender orders were intended to achieve two purposes: preclude Japanese surrender to Chinese Communist troops, and minimize the Soviet occupation role in China and Japan.

Immediately, on August 16, the Soviet Union protested that these surrender provisions violated the Yalta agreements. Stalin demanded that the Soviet surrender zone include the Kuriles and Hokkaido (the northern sector of Japan). Unwilling to cede the means of a Soviet military presence in Japan, Truman on August 18 acceded to the Soviet request for the Kuriles but not for Hokkaido. At the same time he pressed for an American air base on the Kuriles, asserting that it was essential for U.S. commercial and military supply flights to Japan. In a sharp rejoinder on August 22, Stalin reiterated his earlier demand for Hokkaido and opposed Truman's request for an air base on the Kuriles.

This conflict over the status of the Kuriles and Hokkaido was not mere territorial matter; it involved the more basic question of the Truman administration's policy toward the Soviet occupation of Japan. At issue was whether the administration would formally renege on Roosevelt's commitments and whether it was prepared to reject accommodation for a course of confrontation. Although it achieved its objective of precluding Soviet involvement in Japan, the administration hesitated to reject the prospect of a negotiated settlement. Thus Truman adopted a conciliatory tone in replying to Stalin's sharp note on August 25. The United States, he affirmed, had not sought air base but only landing rights on the Kuriles. Denying that such a request was interventionist, as Stalin had charged, Truman further pointed out that the Kuriles were not Soviet territory. Yalta had only permitted Soviet occupation of the islands, he said; their final status would have to be determined at a future peace conference. On August 30 Stalin acceded to the request for landing rights. He denied, however, that the status of the Kuriles was unclear, contending that the cession had been permanent and that future peace talks would merely ratify this fact.

DESPITE ITS SUCCESS in keeping the Soviets out of Japan, the Truman administration failed to avert Soviet involvement in China or to exclude her from the Kuriles. Directly or indirectly, these objectives underlay the shift in administration policy toward the Yalta agreements. This shift necessitated a certain element of duplicity because Truman and Byrnes cunningly, but shortsightedly, sought to have it both ways: they tried to avert the effect of the agreements without formally repudiating or renegotiating them.

It was this clearly contradictory policy that required the administration to refrain from publishing the Yalta agreements on the Far East. To have published them, after all, would have bound the administration to fulfilling them, and this it was not prepared to do. Whereas the Roosevelt administration had published secret agreements when propitious (for example, the three votes and veto agreements in March), the Truman administration neglected to publish the Far

Eastern agreements on three ostensibly favorable occasions: when the Soviet Union declared war on Japan on August 8, when the Sino-Soviet treaty was announced on August 14, or when Soviet troops occupied the Kurile islands on August 27.

Although several newspapers and columnists did suggest that the Soviet actions of August 8 and 14 were related to decisions made at Yalta, for the most part these events were accepted at face value. The United States troop withdrawal that permitted Soviet occupation of the Kuriles, however, precipitated bitter protests by conservatives in both Congress and the press. Soviet possession of these "strategic" islands, it was charged, would directly threaten the security of the United States and Japan.

In a September 4 press conference on the eve of his departure for the London Foreign Ministers Conference, Secretary of State Byrnes attempted to allay this protest by clarifying the reasons for U.S. withdrawal. The decision leading up to it, he told the press, had resulted from "discussions" (as opposed to "agreements," he implied) conducted at Yalta, not Potsdam. Having distinguished the responsibility for the "discussions" as Roosevelt's not Truman's, Byrnes maintained that his attendance at Yalta had provided him with "full" knowledge of these discussions. He then announced his intention to review them at London; a final agreement on the status of the Kuriles, he concluded, could only be made at a forthcoming peace conference.

Byrnes's statements at this press conference were to have serious political ramifications for the Truman administration. By not publishing the Yalta agreements immediately after Byrnes made his disclosures, the administration left itself open to charges of deceit and subversion of the democratic process. The agreements would have been generally accepted by the American public in September. Trust of the Soviet Union was still in force; the Sino-Soviet treaty was being praised (even by Henry Luce's magazines); and, despite conservative criticism, Soviet occupation of the Kuriles was by and large considered a necessary check upon Japan. Furthermore, not disclosing the Yalta agreements earlier remained defensible on military grounds in September; afterward it did not.

Byrnes had been duplicitous in two respects in September: first, in implying that the status of the Kuriles had not yet been defined; and, second, in failing to report the existence of the other Far Eastern agreements. His secretiveness on the latter point stemmed from the administration's desire to avert the Soviets gaining a controlling role in the occupation of Japan by precluding the establishment of an Allied occupation commission. This objective necessarily conflicted with Soviet policy and underlay the atmosphere of distrust that prevailed during the September meetings of the Council of Foreign Ministers in London. Although Soviet Foreign Minister Molotov protested the unilateral character of U.S. occupation policy in Japan, specifically demanding the establishment of an Allied control commission, Byrnes, equivocating, pressed for time. In the end, he succeeded in postponing any final decision on Japan.

The Truman administration's public position on Soviet-American relations involving Japan was in direct contrast to the spirit of conflict and distrust in London. During a September 26 press conference, the President denied that the Soviet Union was dissatisfied with occupation policy toward Japan. When asked whether the Soviet Union had specifically pressed for the establishment of an Allied control commission, he refused to comment; his only knowledge on the matter, he added, came from what he read in the press.

§❧

THIS DUPLICITY about Japan, and the attendant necessity not to publish the Far Eastern agreements—or even, for that matter, admit their existence—seriously compromised the administration's position. The first hint that the agreements did indeed exist occurred during the controversy surrounding the November 1945 resignation of Patrick Hurley as United States Ambassador to China. In resigning, Hurley charged that United States foreign policy had been subverted by "imperialists" and "communists" in both the State Department and the Foreign Service. Having created a national furor, Hurley's resignation and subsequent charges led to special hearings by the Senate Foreign Relations Committee in December. Very quickly these hearings moved from Hurley's charges to the Yalta Far Eastern agreements.

The tone of the Committee's questioning of Hurley was sharp, at times even hostile. Attempting to defend Hurley, who had reiterated his charges of employee disloyalty and insubordination, a sympathetic Senator Styles Bridges (Republican, New Hampshire) asked whether at Yalta—given the absence of Chinese representatives—any agreement concerning China had been concluded. Although he had not attended the conference, Hurley conceded knowledge about the China discussions. He added that Secretary of State Byrnes was a better authority on that subject.

Having already been invited to testify before the Committee, Byrnes appeared the next day. In his prepared statement he dismissed Hurley's charges against the personnel of the State Department and Foreign Service as wholly unfounded. Senator Bridges, however, was much more concerned with the Truman administration's China policy. Repeating his question of the day before, he asked Byrnes whether any agreement concerning China was concluded at Yalta in the absence and without the consent of Chiang Kai-shek.

Bridges' confident tone, and the possibility that he had secured access to the Yalta text through Hurley or another source in the State Department, complicated Byrnes's reply. To admit that agreements had been concluded at Yalta without advising or consulting Chiang would expose the administration's duplicity. Faced with this political dilemma, Byrnes neither affirmed nor denied that an agreement had been made:

> I do not recall the various agreements [of the Yalta Conference]. It is entirely possible that some of the agreements arrived at at Yalta affected China some way or another, and I have told you that I would gladly furnish you the communiqué and then you could decide whether or not they affected China. If they were made they certainly were made by the heads of government and certainly only the three Governments were represented there.

Byrnes had outmaneuvered Bridges by in effect implying ignorance of any China agreements. Bridges then turned the tables, though inadvertently, on both Byrnes and the administration by observing that, had any agreement on China been concluded, the Secretary could not have been unaware of its existence. Thus, at the time when the administration was forced to make the Far Eastern agreements public, it would have to offer a convincing rationale, not only for its earlier failure to publish the agreements, but now for Byrnes's seeming ignorance on the matter as well.

This situation came to pass in February 1946. The event precipitating the publication of the Far Eastern agreements was the Truman administration's announcement in January that it had turned over to an international trusteeship certain Pacific islands captured by the United States from Japan during World War II. During a January 22 press conference, Acting Secretary of State Dean Acheson was asked whether the Soviet Union would similarly be required to turn over the Kuriles to an international trusteeship. In answer, Acheson pointed out that the Yalta agreements had provided only for Soviet occupation of the Kuriles, not a permanent cession of territory; the final disposition would have to be determined at a future peace conference. Acheson conceded, however, that such a conference might simply affirm Soviet control.

Soviet authorities immediately challenged Acheson's remarks. On January 26 Moscow Radio charged that, contrary to Acheson's contention, the Kuriles and South Sakhalin had been ceded to the Soviet Union at Yalta. Moscow specifically denied that Soviet control of these territories was temporary or that Soviet occupation was related only to the prosecution of the war against Japan.

Secretary of State Byrnes was thus forced to tell the truth about Far Eastern agreements concluded at Yalta at a January 29 press conference. The Kuriles and South Sakhalin had in fact been ceded to the Soviet Union at Yalta, he announced; moreover, agreements concerning Port Arthur and Dairen had also been concluded. But these agreements would become binding only after the formal conclusion of a peace treaty with Japan.

The most dramatic aspect of Byrnes's press conference was not the disclosure of the agreements themselves but his attempts to explain the Truman administration's earlier failure to release them or indeed even admit their existence. Byrnes's position was complicated by three factors. First, he *had* attended the Yalta Conference. Second, in September he had publicly expressed knowledge of the "full" Yalta discussion. Third, in December he had indirectly denied that any agreement concerning China had been concluded at Yalta.

What Byrnes did was tell the press that, while a delegate to Yalta, he had left the conference on the afternoon of February 10, before the concluding session the next day. Thus he had not learned about the specifics of the Yalta Far Eastern agreements until August 1945, a few days after the Japanese surrender. In response to further questions, Byrnes said he did not know whether former Secretary of State Edward Stettinius knew about the agreements or where, in fact, the text of them was. It was not, he said, in the State Department archives, but it might be deposited in the White House files.

Once again, Byrnes had adroitly covered his tracks. He

had shifted responsibility for both the Yalta agreements and
the failure to publish them to the Roosevelt administration's
tactics of secrecy. His statement did, however, raise two
important questions. First, had the agreements been privately
concluded by Roosevelt without the knowledge of other
White House or State Department personnel? And, second,
where was the text?

During a January 31 press conference, President Truman
sought to resolve these questions. The text, he claimed, had
always been in the White House files, except when under review either by members of the White House staff or other
administration personnel. While he had always known the
whereabouts of the text, Truman said, he had not reviewed it
until he began to prepare for the Potsdam Conference. When
asked when the agreements would in fact be published, he
answered that it would be necessary first to consult the British
and the Russians. Most of the agreements, he added, had already been made public; the others would be disclosed at the
"proper" time.

THE REASON BEHIND the Truman administration's refraining
for so long from publishing the Yalta Far Eastern agreements
had long-range domestic and international implications. On
the one hand, the administration could not admit that it had
sought to repudiate the agreements by not publishing them insofar as its post-1945 public position had been one of faithful
adherence to those agreements. On the other hand, the administration contended, it had been the Soviets who had all
along consistently shown bad faith.

Thus administration tactics further strained the already uneasy relations between the United States and the Soviet Union.
While Soviet doubts about placing trust in the United States
were strengthened, the Soviet counter-response only served to

further confirm Truman's suspicions about the Soviet Union. This process of mutual distrust being continually reinforced, and the tendency to perceive one's own actions as legitimate and the other nation's as hostile, contributed greatly to the rigid and moralistic tone of the Cold War.

Domestically, the administration's secrecy and duplicity only furthered popular doubts and suspicions about everything and everyone connected with the Yalta Conference. Moreover, they legitimated the McCarthyites' contention that, since Roosevelt's "secret" diplomacy at Yalta—a brand of diplomacy continued by Truman—had contributed to the "loss" of China, Congress must reassert its authority and restrain the executive branch. Administration secrecy in the instance of initially withholding publication of the Wedemeyer Report and the secret conduct of the Marshall Mission only increased the effect of the McCarthyites' charges.

There had to be, conservative Congressmen now claimed, an extensive congressional review of past policy decisions to uncover the "full" secrets of Yalta and to expose and dismiss those who had acted disloyally. Only Congress could do this.

5

The Quest for
Absolute Security

THE CHANGED RHETORIC of postwar foreign policy begat a
popular obsession for achieving a total victory over communism—or, what was much the same thing in the eyes of
most Americans, the Soviet Union. The failure to do so, the
then current reasoning went, would directly threaten American liberties and, in addition, subvert the American mission
of moral leadership in the world. Accordingly, the Truman
administration's foreign policy came to be judged in terms of
its effectiveness in meeting the threat of communism. Since
postwar rhetoric also popularized the theme of American
omnipotence, it came to be believed that an American victory
was inevitable—inevitable, that is, so long as the country
possessed the necessary will and resolve. The Soviet threat
per se was not considered major; Soviet gains were thought
merely the result of administration errors or inaction.

In any event, such reasoning provided the basis for the belief that both the Roosevelt and Truman administrations had
"lost" China and "given" Eastern Europe to the Soviet Union.
It also informed popular reactions to the Soviet Union's successful atomic bomb testing (September 1949). Despite the
fact that the United States retained superiority in the stock-
piling of atomic weapons, the loss of its atomic monopoly

severely shocked and frightened those Americans who had come to view—not without administration prodding—this monopoly as the sole guarantee of national security. In part, this reaction explains the support, admittedly among a minority of Americans, for a preventive attack on the Soviet Union before she could develop nuclear weapons of her own. More importantly, however, Americans came to believe that the Soviets' development of an atomic bomb came about neither through Soviet science nor technology, but had simply been stolen by Soviet spies.

The result was an obsessive national fear of subversion. The real threat to America's security was now believed to come from betrayals on the part of disloyal federal employees. Nor were these employees viewed as mere reformers and radicals, as the Dies and Thomas Committees had charged, but as actual foreign agents. This was Senator McCarthy's refinement on earlier charges.

The McCarthyites' post-1950 attack on the Truman administration centered on the subversive character of former New Deal personnel, who used their important jobs to betray the national interest. Dismissing the notion that certain administration decisions had been simply errors in judgment, McCarthy and his supporters instead charged that decisions so inimical to American ideals and the national interest could only have been formulated by communists or pro-communists. Recent exposures of actual espionage served only to confirm the existence of a real internal-security threat. Had not the "traitor" Alger Hiss attended the Yalta Conference and participated in the "sell-out" of China and Eastern Europe? Had not lax State Department security procedures, as in the *Amerasia* case, enabled Soviet "agents" to secure national secrets? Had not Ethel and Julius Rosenberg helped Soviet agents steal the atomic bomb? Had not Judith Coplon secured a loyalty clearance and subsequently stolen FBI classified material for the Soviet Union?

The ostensibly documented nature of the McCarthyites'
charges greatly enhanced their popular acceptance. While
Senator McCarthy's own estimates varied from time to time,
the precision of his reference to eighty-one (not eighty or
eighty-five) security risks in the State Department and his
contention that he had "in his right hand" evidence docu-
menting his accusations were supremely convincing. In reality,
of course, McCarthy never did provide serious evidence of an
internal-security threat, nor did he or his supporters propose
any measures that might effectively combat future espionage.
In the main, theirs was only a search-and-destroy operation,
but one with just enough of the ring of truth to it to make it
effective, given the already established popular distrust of the
Truman administration.

By 1950 many Americans believed that the Truman administration's loyalty procedures were inadequate to the problem of internal subversion. This belief was not based on any
solid evidence of an operating Soviet spy ring, but derived
from isolated, though dramatic, incidents: the *Amerasia* case;
the Canadian Royal Commission disclosure; the Alger Hiss,
Julius and Ethel Rosenberg, and Judith Coplon cases. In
two of these instances, the Judith Coplon and *Amerasia* cases,
conviction of the accused "agents" was frustrated on the
procedural grounds that the FBI had resorted to unconstitutional acts in obtaining evidence or information leading
to arrests. Neither case, moreover, despite the way they were
dealt with in the press, posed a serious threat to the national
security.

Even though nothing even faintly resembling an extensive
espionage ring had been uncovered, the impact of these two
cases on the public was sensational. In part, it resulted from
publicity put out by the Department of Justice, which saw in
these cases an opportunity to secure legislation to strengthen
its own investigatory procedures. For his part, President Truman neither counteracted the Justice Department's tactics nor

fully informed the public about how limited were the threats that these cases actually posed to national security. On the contrary, his rhetoric and his actions only intensified fears of Soviet subversion. Truman claimed that traditional security methods did not adequately safeguard the nation against the communist threat. Consequently, it soon came to be believed that only the most elaborate security arrangements could save the nation. Now not only nuclear scientists but janitors and gardeners were suspect. The really insidious aspect of Truman's rhetoric about loyalty and the McCarthyites' cries of betrayal was that it encouraged a popular mania for absolute security that extended beyond the prosecution of overt acts of disloyalty to a suspicion of all potentially subversive ideas.

By 1950 the administration's announced quest for absolute security had rendered it vulnerable to attacks on its own existing loyalty procedures. The public had been educated to believe in the necessity for total security. Given these stringent demands, any subversion whatsoever came to be construed as the result only of inherent government incompetence or deliberate treason. The Truman administration had no intention of establishing an effective internal-security program, the McCarthyites charged, because it was ignorant of communist espionage methods; indeed, only a full and public investigation of the matter by Congress would result in the adoption of proper safeguards. When the administration reaffirmed in 1950 its decision of two years earlier to restrict congressional access to FBI loyalty reports, it only enabled McCarthy and other congressional conservatives to assail that decision as an attempt to cover-up.

THE PRESIDENT'S DECISION on March 22, 1947, to establish a permanent employee loyalty program merely reinforced popular fears about the existence of a serious threat to national security. Moreover, the program legitimized the idea of judging an employee's loyalty on the basis of his previous associations, activities, and beliefs. Although it attempted to provide definite safeguards against unfounded or unsubstantiated accusations, the administration's insistence on *effective* protection against disloyalty provided, potentially, a rationale for abusing individual rights.

Nor were the loyalty program's objectives clearly defined. Before it was instituted, the dismissal of an employee on the grounds of disloyalty had required definite proof. Such dismissals as occurred had been confined to the military and diplomatic sectors of the federal government. Truman, however, established the loyalty program not simply to penalize overt acts of disloyalty but—and this is where clarity was most seriously lacking—to preclude *all possible* subversion: his goal was absolute security. Accordingly, the standard for dismissal for disloyalty became: "reasonable grounds exist for the belief that the person involved is disloyal to the Government of the United States." Furthermore, *all* federal employees, regardless of the nature of their jobs, were to be investigated. Because past associations and activities were one of the "reasonable grounds" for dismissal, certain actions, beliefs, or associations became stigmatized or were sufficient grounds for dismissal. Thus the loyalty program, particularly in its provision for a listing of suspect organizations by the Attorney General, established a simple, and by no means accurate, litmus test for loyalty.

Once the loyalty program was implemented, department and agency heads were given the responsibility for making dismissals. Yet since they themselves were often chiefly concerned with averting any future disclosures, which might raise questions about their zeal in ferreting out "communists," evidence that would not have held up in any court was sometimes sufficient to result in a loyalty hearing—and, in a few cases, in the dismissal of an employee. With these administrative officers running the program, the routine dismissal or resignation of certain employees, along with the compilation of loyalty files containing derogatory information, tended further to confirm the existence of a real internal-security problem. Finally, the simple existence of the loyalty program fostered demands that it function: that department and agency heads aggressively seek out and dismiss "disloyal" employees.

When the program came under attack for not achieving absolute loyalty, the limited safeguards to individual liberties originally written into it were further circumscribed. Thus, in April 1951, in an effort to expedite dismissals, the administration amended the dismissal provision to read: "reasonable doubt as to the loyalty of the individual involved to the Government of the United States." By replacing "grounds" with "doubt," and "disloyal[ty]" with "loyalty," the amendment subordinated individual rights to internal security, and internal security itself to internal suspicion.

§●

THE EFFECT OF the loyalty program in intensifying popular anxieties about subversion was immediate. As early as November 1946, when Truman appointed a Temporary Commission on Employee Loyalty to ascertain the quality of existing national-security safeguards, the public was confronted with the possibility of a dire threat to American freedom. In its report to the President, the Commission gave what it believed to be urgent reasons for the adoption of a loyalty program:

> The presence within the government of *any* disloyal or subversive persons, or the *attempt* by *any* such person to *obtain employment,* presents a problem of *such importance* that it must be dealt with vigorously and effectively [italics added].

The Commission went on to say:

> . . . The employment of disloyal or subversive persons presents more than a speculative threat to our system of government, it [the Commission] is unable, based on facts presented to it, to state how far-reaching that threat is. Certainly, the recent Canadian Espionage exposure, the Communist Party line activities of some of the leaders and some of the members of a government organization, and current disclosures of disloyal employees provide sufficient evidence to convince a fair-minded person that a threat exists.

The Commission's views reflected the priorities of both Attorney General Tom Clark and President Truman, the two men most directly involved in the execution and development of the loyalty program. In fact, Clark's views on subversion and security went well beyond those of the Commission. In his testimony before the Commission, Clark outlined his conception of the loyalty problem:

> The problem of subversive or disloyal persons in the government is a most serious one. While the number of such persons has not as yet reached serious proportions, there is no doubt that the *presence* of *any* in the Government service or the *possibility* of their entering Government service are serious matters, and should cause the gravest concern to those charged with the responsibility of solving the problem. I do not believe the gravity of the problem should be weighed in the light of numbers, but rather from the view of the *serious threat which even one disloyal person constitutes to the security of the Government of the United States* [italics added].

The same confident assurances that failure to prevent the employment of potentially disloyal men and women would result in a grave crisis also dominated Truman's statements. Indeed, his Executive Order 9835, prescribing the procedures for administering the loyalty program, specifically stipulated:

> Whereas each employee of the Government of the United States is endowed with a measure of trusteeship over the

democratic processes which are the heart and sinew of the United States; and

Whereas it is of vital importance that persons employed in the Federal Service be of complete and unswerving loyalty to the United States; and

Whereas, although the loyalty of by far the overwhelming majority of all Government employees is beyond question, the *presence* within the Government service of *any* disloyal or subversive person constitutes a threat to our democratic processes; and

Whereas maximum protection must be afforded the United States against infiltration of disloyal persons into the ranks of its employees, and equal protection from unfounded accusations of disloyalty must be afforded to loyal employees of the Government. [Italics added.]

As the basic rationale for the government's loyalty program, these conclusions by Truman clearly obviated the need for any restrained assessment of what constituted a realistic threat to the national security. Together, Truman, Clark, and the Commission suggested that any individual in government, no matter what his job, might threaten the national security. Such hyperbolic reasoning was hardly likely to provide the basis for a responsible loyalty program. In more realistic terms, only those employees who had direct access to security information could conceivably engage in effective subversion. Any threat these people might pose could be counteracted not by a sweeping loyalty program but simply by restricting employment in sensitive agencies or instituting tighter surveillance within these agencies. But instead of this, the Truman administration acted on the premise that the presence of any subversive government employee seriously threatened the national security, which of course ultimately redounded greatly to Senator McCarthy's advantage.

Of equal advantage to McCarthy was the fact that the administration had publicly defined the loyalty program's objective as the attainment of absolute security. Yet even after the loyalty program was instituted, men and women of dubious loyalty, as in the past, continued in the government's employ. In the view of the public, Alger Hiss, William Remington, Judith Coplon, and the Rosenbergs tended to confirm what was felt to be the inadequacies of the Truman administration's loyalty procedures. The case of John Stewart Service, who had initially secured a loyalty clearance and who was later dismissed after bitter McCarthyite denunciations, seemed further documentation of the imperfections of the loyalty program. Service had been implicated in the *Amerasia* case and as a consequence had been subjected to six different loyalty checks as a Foreign Service officer, all of which had resulted in his clearance. The existence of derogatory information in his loyalty file, the public knowledge of his involvement in *Amerasia,* and his disdain for the Nationalist regime in China, made him a persistent example in McCarthy's denunciation of the administration's loyalty procedures. When Service was denied clearance in 1951 (the seventh time around), the inadequacy of the earlier loyalty program was apparently confirmed.

THE PRESIDENT'S Executive Order directing the Attorney General to draft a list of subversive organizations also benefited the McCarthyites by exacerbating public fears. Although the President's order specifically stated that the mere fact of membership in an organization on the list would not in itself be sufficient grounds for denying an employee loyalty clearance, it imposed no restrictions on the Attorney General's power to list any organization he chose. Despite the fact that a listed organization had the right to appeal its being on the list, Truman's failure to require either more exacting procedures of classification or open hearings before the list was finally composed gave the Attorney General's list, at least in the public mind, authority as *the* definitive report on subversive organizations. In fact, the Attorney General's list, which was composed without establishing time limits for its findings nor assuring due process to accused organizations, came to be popularly understood as a proscription of the treasonable activity of the listed organizations. From here it required only the smallest step to believing that any person who had ever belonged to an organization on the list was capable of, if not firmly committed to, subversion. Since many federal employees had, for a variety of reasons, belonged to one or another of these organizations in the 1930's, the administration had, quite without intention, declared an anti-radical field day on former Roosevelt and present Truman administration personnel.

By resolving doubts about employee loyalty in favor of the government, the revised dismissal standard put into effect in 1951 widened the scope of loyalty investigations. The original standard had protected federal employees by requiring evidence of disloyalty to go beyond mere suspicion, and by stipulating, in addition, that membership in suspect organizations could not alone justify dismissal. But the more security-conscious among the administration found this restricting. As early as 1949, both Seth Richardson, chairman of the Loyalty Review Board (the agency established by Truman's Executive Order within the Civil Service Commission to provide a final review of the decisions of departmental loyalty boards), and the Department of Justice were urging the President to tighten employee dismissal standards. Committed to maximizing surveillance, both agencies wanted a standard whose basic premise was that federal employment was a privilege, not a right. Accordingly, any doubts whatsoever about the individual should, even in the absence of conclusive evidence, be sufficient to bring about his dismissal. The Justice Department and the Loyalty Review Board persistently emphasized that a real threat to national security would continue to exist as long as individuals of "doubtful" loyalty, and therefore "potential" danger, were retained in federal employment. They thus argued that the original dismissal standard had to be revised. Ultimately, in response to this pressure, and along with it the heightened security consciousness that emerged with the Cold War, Truman acceded to the demand to revise the standard. On April 28, 1951, by Executive Order 10241, he amended the dismissal standard to preclude the employment of persons "who are potentially disloyal or who are bad security risks."

In the end, the concept of "potential" disloyalty harnessed to the contention that federal employment was a privilege and not a right worked against the administration. For one thing, it further exaggerated the extent of the internal threat to national security. For another, it increased the number of federal employees who were dismissed—some after previous clearance. It also caused a great many job applications to be denied. More than any single act of subversion, it helped document, for those who were ready to believe in conspiracy to begin with, the success of communist infiltration in the federal service.

ALTHOUGH THE Truman administration consistently declared it wanted to balance the task of rooting out disloyal employees with establishing safeguards insuring the fair treatment of the unjustly accused, in actual practice the former took precedence. Administration rhetoric about safeguards notwithstanding, before the McCarthyite assault the administration had not seemed much concerned about the effect of its loyalty procedures on individual rights. In 1948 Truman had castigated the investigations of the House Un-American Activities Committee and the proposed Mundt-Nixon bill as potentially undermining the Bill of Rights. His main emphasis then, however, had been partisan: he questioned whether

HUAC was interested in uncovering communists or New Dealers. In 1948, too, the Department of Justice proposed an alternative to the bill introduced by Mundt and Nixon and instituted the prosecution of American Communist party leaders under the Smith Act. But once the McCarthyites began criticizing the loyalty program in the 1950's, demanding permission to review the loyalty reports, or in some instances the dismissal of suspect employees, Truman adopted a civil libertarian posture. He then contended that summary dismissal as well as congressional access to the loyalty reports might transgress individual rights. Yet the only effect of this response was to make him seem duplicitous. After all, the issue raised by McCarthy and his congressional supporters— and it was never directly challenged by the administration— was not the necessity of the loyalty program itself but the effectiveness of its procedures. Rooting out subversives, not individual civil liberties, was the primary consideration.

In fact, the administration's earlier obsession with absolute security had already caused it to impinge upon individual rights (and impartial justice). This was accomplished by the very act of compiling loyalty reports in the first place. When the loyalty program was first instituted, the FBI was directed to investigate all incumbent federal employees. If during its initial investigation the FBI uncovered information that raised doubts about the loyalty of an employee, it would then institute a full field investigation. In both investigations, the initial and full field, the FBI made no serious effort to ascertain the accuracy of the information it received. Its final report simply included all charges against an individual, both solicited and unsolicited, verified and unverified. As such, these reports were a curious admixture of unsubstantiated charges by private citizens and information secured by the FBI investigative staff. Much of the data was wholly unfounded; some of the private testimony was slanderous; and most of the contents of these reports would not have been accepted as evidence in a court of law. Yet the FBI evaluated or weighed none of this information. Its rationale for not doing so was that all accusations, even unsubstantiated ones, might prove helpful to future investigations and that its own responsibility was to uncover as much information about an employee as possible.

The FBI demanded that its loyalty reports be kept secret. As an investigatory agency examining the past activities and beliefs of suspect employees, thè FBI felt it had to guarantee the confidential nature of its sources of information. There were pragmatic reasons for doing so. Publication of the reports might "dry up" these sources; publication could also prove helpful to persons under suspicion or review. In addition, the distinctly conservative bias of the information and charges contained in the FBI's reports might lend support to civil libertarian attacks on the FBI, and thus undermine the image of nonpartisan professionalism that J. Edgar Hoover sought to create for his organization.

Truman went along with the FBI demands in 1947, stipulating that: "The reports and other investigative material developed by the investigative department or agency shall be retained by such department or agency in each case." In accordance with this restriction, Attorney General Tom Clark, on July 8, 1947, directed all Department of Justice employees not to honor requests from other agencies or committees for information obtained from FBI sources. All such requests, the Attorney General ordered, should be referred to his office for approval.

The Attorney General's directive and Truman's Executive Order did not, however, restrict congressional access to department loyalty files. That restriction was imposed on March 14, 1948, by another presidential Executive Order. Only the President, Truman then directed, could approve congressional requests for department loyalty reports. He cited three justifications for this procedure: (1) that the confidential nature of the reports demanded executive independence from the legislature; (2) that disclosure of FBI sources might prejudice further investigations and hence the national security; and (3) that innocent employees had to be protected from public exposure of unfounded or unsubstantiated charges.

Despite its authoritarian nature, this Executive Order was aimed primarily at preventing the equally authoritarian House Committee on Un-American Activities from exploiting the investigative reputation and resources of the FBI by quoting publicly from its reports.* As in 1947, Truman's order did not, however, detail the partial inaccuracy or unreliability of the reports. This omission served, on the one hand, to corroborate and lend substance to largely unsubstantiated charges; on the other, it enabled the McCarthyites to center their attack not on the nature of the evidence but on the rationale for the administration's refusal to cooperate with an independent (non-executive) examination of the reports.†

Coupled with the administration's insistence on the confidential nature of the FBI reports, the continued employment of such men as William Remington, Edward Condon, John Davies, John Carter Vincent, and John Stewart Service, all

* In hearings during 1947 and early 1948 the Committee, under the chairmanship of J. Parnell Thomas (Republican, New Jersey), had sought to discredit the New Deal by establishing the subversive character of federal personnel. A similar attempt was made by a Subcommittee of the Senate Appropriations Committee under the chairmanship of Homer Ferguson (Republican, Michigan).

† In fact, the administration's withholding of the FBI evidence worked to the McCarthyites' advantage: by reading excerpts from State Department loyalty files (obtained from sources within the State Department, the FBI, or the House Committee of Appropriations, which investigated the State Department in 1948), conservative Congressmen could produce evidence of disloyalty that seemed to come from the FBI itself. And so the administration's action seemed to be no more than an effort to cover up a serious threat to national security under the guise of confidentiality.

of whose loyalty reports contained damaging information, raised popular concern about administration priorities. Why were these men not dismissed? Why had they been employed to begin with? Why had they not been prosecuted? Was the resort to confidentiality only a resort to treason? Certainly, the disclosures that had led to the trial of Alger Hiss constituted one serious administration failure to act upon information supplied by the FBI. HUAC repeatedly pointed out that the Truman administration, though it had had unrestricted access to the FBI's report on Hiss, had neither dismissed Hiss nor prosecuted him until forced to do so by *public* revelations of the Committee's hearings. How many other spies lurked in the government under what amounted to the administration's protection?

Despite such criticism from the McCarthyites in Congress, the Truman administration continued to refuse to release the FBI reports for congressional scrutiny. Truman outlined the basic arguments against doing so in a letter of March 28, 1950, to Senator Millard Tydings (Democrat, Maryland). The letter was subsequently released to the press. Denying Tydings' request for the investigative files of the eighty-one alleged State Department employees accused by Senator McCarthy of being communists, Truman explained:

> The public disclosure of F.B.I. reports will reveal investigative procedures and techniques. If publicized, criminals, foreign agents, subversives, and others would thus be forewarned and seek ways and means of carrying out their activities, thus avoiding detection and hampering the efficiency of an investigative agency. The underground operations of criminals and subversives already are most difficult of detection, and I do not believe the security of the Nation would be furthered by applying any additional shackles to the F.B.I.
>
> . . . To make public F.B.I. reports would be to break confidence, and persons interviewed in the future might be even more reluctant to furnish information. . . .

A public disclosure of F.B.I. reports would reveal the identity of sources of information, and, in some cases, at least, would place in jeopardy the lives of confidential sources of information.

Truman's stance was unconvincing and, because it was, proved to be politically disastrous. First, McCarthy's principal source for his charges was in fact information contained in the reports. Second, the identity of sources could after all easily be concealed by careful editing; Congressmen were as unlikely as the President to violate their confidential nature. Third, the substance of McCarthyite demands centered not on the sources of information but on the contents of the reports. Fourth, if considerations of national security were so fundamental, then the administration should not have allowed the Subcommittee of the House Committee on Appropriations to review State Department loyalty reports in 1947–1948. Fifth, it was argued that the administration did not really want to aid the FBI, since not publishing its findings only hampered its investigative work. Thus the McCarthyites, charging that only through congressional scrutiny could solid investigations be achieved, emerged as the champions of the FBI.

The President's Executive Order of September 25, 1951, extending "national security" classification restrictions to all federal agencies, only intensified popular mistrust of administration secrecy. Truman denied that the new classification requirements constituted censorship of the press; nor, he said, were they intended to cover up administration mistakes. He had extended classification, he maintained, only to keep the nation's military secrets from falling into enemy hands. Previous classification restrictions confined to the State and Defense Departments had become inadequate; now every agency and department with access to classified information had to be restricted. Truman added: "I do not believe that the best solution [to the problem of protecting national secrets while still insuring public access to legitimate sources] can be reached by adopting an approach based on the theory that everyone has a right to know our military secrets and related information concerning the national security."

Subsequent administration defenses of the new restrictions —specifically, the contention that too much information was being released—increased the outcries against the President's Executive Order. In seeking to discredit his critics, Truman accused them of passing up "the opportunity to serve the cause of freedom of information in the dangerous days ahead when the safety of our country and the freedom for which it stands are in peril. . . . We can only win in the present struggle if we all work together." On the one hand, this rhetoric heightened popular fears of subversion; on the other, it supported the plea for congressional surveillance of the executive branch of government itself. The popular feeling was that unity and obedience were not half so necessary to the nation's well-being as documentation that the administration was capable of protecting the national security. In fact, by 1951 it appeared that that security could best be protected by more information, not additional restrictions.

RHETORICAL ANTI-COMMUNISM was central to the Truman administration's political posture from 1948 on; the standard for judging every policy proposal put forth became the degree of its anti-communist thrust. In 1948, for example, Truman asserted that no one "who believes in the destruction of our form of government" should be permitted to teach children. Similarly, he affirmed that "communists shall not work for the government and our vigilance shall be unremitting." Without clearly defining real threats—or perhaps simply because they failed to—these pronouncements implied that certain beliefs were so dangerous that any measure taken to restrict them was justified.

Certainly, this view was widely held. Since 1947 the conservatives in Congress had been seeking enactment of legislation outlawing, or at a minimum requiring registration of membership in, the Communist party. Led by Karl Mundt and Richard Nixon, this campaign was initially stymied in part by opposition from both conservatives (Robert A. Taft and J. Edgar Hoover, among them) and moderates (Thomas E. Dewey). Arguing on constitutional and pragmatic grounds, these men insisted that any legislation enacted to provide surveillance of, and to impose restrictions upon, the activities of the Communist party had at the same time to uphold the civil libertarian principles of the Constitution.

Legislative proposals brought before Congress in 1949, however, included not only Mundt's and Nixon's measure—plus a similar one introduced by Senator Homer Ferguson—but a bill originally drafted by the Department of Justice in 1947. Because this measure contained three controversial proposals—the authorization of wiretapping, registration of Communist party members, and the imposition of strict penalties for unauthorized disclosures of classified information—it had consistently been denied Budget clearance on the grounds of outraging civil liberties.* Despite this opposition, however, the Department of Justice had continued to lobby the measure through consultations with interested Congressmen and committee chairmen, the most enthusiastic of whom was Senator Pat McCarran (Democrat, Nevada), the chairman of the Judiciary Committee.

* Before submission to Congress as an executive bill, any department-proposed measure first had to secure clearance from the Bureau of the Budget that it was consistent with the program outlined by the President in his State of the Union address. The Budget Bureau not only reviewed the Justice Department proposal but submitted it for the consideration of other interested agencies and departments.

Before the outbreak of the Korean War, in early 1950, McCarran had pressured the President and the Democratic congressional leadership for early Senate consideration of the Justice bill. Because internal-security legislation was not then a White House priority, the administration did not honor his request. The Korean War, however, drastically changed the political context of the bill by raising doubts about the effectiveness of existing internal-security safeguards. Administration cautions on the war's possible ramifications only added to this concern. It was against this background of war and possible subversion that the McCarthyites demanded the immediate enactment of internal-security legislation. Significantly, Senator McCarran then dropped the Justice bill in favor of a more drastic measure of his own.

The McCarran bill offered the Truman administration the choice of openly opposing the enactment of all internal-security legislation or proposing on its own an alternate bill that would minimize possible abuses of individual rights. Inevitably, this choice required that the administration decide whether to allow the Communist party's activities to be restricted through surveillance. The President eventually determined to adopt a moderate course. He openly opposed the bills of Mundt and Nixon, Ferguson and Olin Johnston, and McCarran on the grounds that they transgressed civil liberties and were symptomatic of unwarranted hysteria. At the same time he proposed an alternate bill, which, while upholding the Constitution, would still protect the national security.

While stressing the gravity of the internal and external threats to national security, Truman emphasized that protection must be achieved without "unduly" limiting individual liberties. Tracing the history of the people's wariness of efforts to restrict civil liberties, Truman specifically raised the historical legacy of the Alien and Sedition Acts—presented in the 1790's ostensibly to protect national security but which effectively impinged upon individual freedoms and dissent.

The lesson of the Alien and Sedition Act controversy, Truman argued, was that "extreme and arbitrary security measures strike at the very heart of our free society, and that we must be eternally vigilant against those who would undermine freedom in the name of security."

In view of the frenzied climate of American politics in 1950, Truman's legislative tactics effectively immobilized his administration's efforts to defeat the McCarran bill. By introducing a rival bill instead of seeking to defeat McCarran's, he undermined his attempt to emphasize the importance of civil libertarian considerations. Indeed, his introduction of an alternate bill only served to affirm an apparent need for more effective legislation. Moreover, Truman's emphasis on civil liberties and vague references to "undue," "excessive," "arbitrary" pressures ran counter to his administration's arguments in support of its own bill.

According to the administration, Soviet aggressive aims, as manifest specifically in the Korean War, confirmed the "clear and present danger" that communism posed to all countries. Because of this danger, the administration maintained that the American Communist party, which was simply an agent of the Soviet Union (and thus of its aggression), could constitutionally be singled out. To control the subversive activities of the party and its front organizations, the administration recommended enacting a registration and report procedure. It did not, however, specifically identify those front organizations; it only vaguely proposed that the Attorney General be empowered to list such organizations.

Attempting to secure passage of its own bill over those advanced by the McCarthyites in Congress, Truman had the Department of Justice draft a statement outlining the reasons for supporting the administration. This statement, its rhetoric reflecting administration strategy, pointed out:

> The following tactical comparison may be made between
> S. 2311 [the measure formally supported by the Republican

congressional leadership] and the proposed substitute. The substitute presents fewer constitutional questions than does S. 2311. The substitute will do one of two things: it will obtain quickly valuable information, and, when in a few months the Supreme Court has decided the Smith Act and Loyalty Order cases, we will have more guidance on the drafting of any further legislation which may be necessary; or, if simple disclosure requirements are going to be defied by some American citizens while others are dying to repel Communist aggression, then we will find that out without going through years of legal proceedings, and the Government can act accordingly.

The Truman administration thus maintained that new legislation was needed to curb potential sabotage; yet, at the same time, it opposed the measure advocated by McCarran by noting the desirability of minimizing possibly unconstitutional procedures. This dichotomy served to undercut the administration's position; the emphasis on the gravity of the security threat contrasted sharply to arguments that the administration bill reduced constitutional objections and that further legislation could be enacted when necessary. Moreover, despite the administration's line that its bill balanced the threat to internal security with the threat to civil liberties, its main thrust had in fact always been that domestic communism posed a very real threat to national security. In his August 1950 message Truman had repeatedly referred to "this period of increasing international difficulty and danger" and had stressed the need to protect American freedoms from "internal as well as external attack."

The President was also operating on politically untenable ground when, on the one hand, he commended past administration security measures and, on the other, suggested that "new circumstances" required certain adjustments of those measures. The argument was particularly unconvincing since the Truman administration had not earlier attempted to exercise leadership to secure these "adjustments," but instead had sought to prevent the enactment of the anti-communist Mundt-Nixon bill and had not in 1948, 1949, or even the spring of 1950 pressed for the enactment of an internal-security bill drafted by the Justice Department. Truman's rhetoric in 1950, describing the security problem confronting the nation, further confounded this crisis in credibility. He thus observed that "today, we face most acutely the threat of the communist movement, international in scope, directed from a central source, and committed to the overthrow of democratic institutions throughout the world." But he then warned against "unwise or excessive security measures" or "undue" restrictions on civil liberties.

These remarks reveal a striking contradiction between administration rhetoric and response. Truman seemed to want to defeat the threat of subversion and yet seemed unwilling to oppose it too strongly. If the threat to the nation *was* as acute as he suggested, and if the American Communist party *was* an agent of an international conspiratorial movement committed to overthrowing democracy, then restrictions on communist activities would be neither "unwise" nor "excessive" but absolutely essential. While internal-security legislation would necessarily violate the liberties of American Communists, such legislation would be eminently justified in view of the Communists' ultimate intent to deny those rights to every non-Communist American. And if innocent individuals suffered from the legislation, even that injustice would be justifiable in light of the larger goal of guaranteeing basic liberties to (almost) all.

Thus the administration's attempts to invoke its own vigilant prosecution of communists—citing the trial and conviction of the United States Communist party leadership under the Smith Act, and the dismissal of "disloyal" federal employees under the loyalty program—at the same time it sought to secure congressional and public support for its essentially libertarian proposal, only succeeded in increasing popular mistrust. If the administration had been as vigilant in the past as it claimed to have been, then neither a new security program was needed, nor were additional security measures required.

At all events, the administration's proposal of an alternative bill failed to prevent congressional enactment of the McCarran bill. Truman was then confronted with the necessity of either signing or vetoing this bill. He vetoed it, but his reasons for doing so again failed either to develop support sufficient for upholding the veto or to create a more tolerant, less emotion-laden political climate. Despite his references to the jeopardy to civil liberties inherent in the McCarran bill, Truman maintained a vigorous anti-communist stance in his veto message—specifically, he denied that the McCarran bill was an effective anti-communist measure:

> It has been claimed over and over again that this is an "anti-Communist" bill—a "communist control" bill. But in actual operation the bill would have results exactly the opposite of those intended.
>
> It would actually weaken our existing internal security measures and would seriously hamper the Federal Bureau of Investigation and other security agencies. . . .
>
> No consideration of expediency can justify the enactment of such a bill as this, a bill which would so greatly weaken our liberties and give aid and comfort to the enemy who would destroy us. I have, therefore, no alternative but to return the bill without my approval and I earnestly request the Congress to reconsider its action.

How could an anti-communist bill aid the communists? Truman's rationale was simply not credible. Apparently, the administration was more concerned with its image than with confronting the communist threat.

By 1950 a real crisis of popular confidence in the Truman administration had arrived. It chief beneficiaries, naturally, were the McCarthyites. Other events and administration decisions in 1950–1951 increased this crisis of confidence: Alger Hiss was convicted of perjury—i.e., falsely denying that he had given secrets to Whittaker Chambers in 1938; William Remington was also convicted of perjury; Judith Coplon, a Department of Justice employee, was charged with stealing FBI secrets for a Soviet agent; John Stewart Service, six times cleared by loyalty boards in preceding years, was denied a loyalty clearance; and the Rosenbergs were tried and convicted of helping steal "the secret" of the atomic bomb for the Soviet Union. After successfully exploding an atomic bomb of their own, the Russians were developing a nuclear stockpile and delivery system. The Korean War had broken out, with the Chinese Communists intervening on the side of North Korea, while the Chinese Nationalists had been denied the right to aid the United Nations forces in Korea or to launch an attack on the Chinese mainland. The administration was accused of refusing fully to utilize American military power to bring about "victory over communism" in Korea.

These developments seemed to reveal the inability, if not the unwillingness, of the Truman administration to meet the communist threat head-on. Buffeted by exaggerated anti-communist rhetoric from both the McCarthyites and the administration, the public demanded an explanation why (apparent) communist subversion (apparently) continued. Only McCarthy and the congressional conservatives proposed a convincing answer: a lack of congressional surveillance and executive commitment to root out subversion. The external and internal threats to national security stemmed ultimately from the same source—"communists in government." American communists and their sympathizers had subverted United States foreign policy and prevented the effective use of American power and influence against communism. By stealing diplomatic secrets, American communists and their sympathizers had expedited the emergence of the Soviet Union as a great atomic power, giving the Soviet Union the secret of the atomic bomb. And these same subversives threatened to betray the country completely by undermining its every political, economic, and religious liberty.

The Truman administration's entire conduct in regard to internal loyalty problems resulted in a fatal loss of confidence. Vigorous action was apparently needed; yet the administration either responded timidly or simply failed to act. Capitalizing on this disparity between administration rhetoric and response, the McCarthyites offered a direct anti-communist offensive which, because it was consistent with the basic premises and rhetoric of the postwar loyalty debate, captured popular support. The irony, of course, was that the debate itself had been shaped by the Truman administration.

6

The Department of Justice
and the Cold War

THE Department of Justice—and in particular Attorneys General Tom C. Clark and J. Howard McGrath and FBI Director J. Edgar Hoover—exercised a strong influence on popular American attitudes during the postwar security debate. In general, the Department's commitment to the investigation and prosecution of would-be subversives made it vehemently anti-communist and, despite its protests to the contrary, relatively indifferent to questions of civil liberties. The Justice Department's repeated warnings about the grave internal-security threat confronting the nation, along with its narrow definition of "proper" loyalty, helped to foster the political climate that ultimately led to the rise of Senator Joseph McCarthy. Although technically responsible to the President, under Clark, McGrath, and Hoover the Justice Department often operated wholly independent of—indeed, sometimes at clear cross-purposes against—the main principles of Truman's policy.

In many instances the Justice Department's priorities were the very ones congressional conservatives later championed. Although the Department and congressional conservatives might differ on tactics, on matters of principle they were in relative agreement. Many Justice Department employees, particularly in the FBI, were so sympathetic with Senator McCarthy's aims that they supplied him with copies or excerpts from the FBI loyalty files on their own initiative. While Attorneys General Clark and McGrath did at times attack McCarthy and his congressional supporters, those attacks were for the most part partisan in motivation. Both before and after 1950 both men worked closely with many congressional conservatives in the effort to enact internal-security legislation.

The Justice Department's internal-security goal was two-fold: to curb "potentially subversive" situations and, at the same time, to institute procedures to expedite prosecution. As such, the Department's concept of subversion was sufficiently broad to be in essence anti-radical; it was, in other words, as much concerned with the political beliefs and affiliations of federal employees as with overt acts of espionage and sabotage. According to the Department, Soviet agents were not its only domestic problem. It also felt the need to awaken the public to the dangers of political radicalism as well as the civil libertarian restrictions imposed on federal investigative agencies.

As EARLY AS 1945 Attorney General Clark and FBI Director Hoover had sought to continue wartime investigative procedures, which had proved expeditious even if they involved transgressing constitutional restrictions on federal powers and individual rights. Concerned over the relaxation of popular concern for internal security after the war, Clark and Hoover demanded continued vigilance, the surveillance of "suspicious activities which may concern national security," and the repatriation of "alien enemies" dangerous to American security. This concern for security went so far that, in October 1946, the Justice Department announced that registration statements would once again be required of agents of Allied governments who during World War II had been freed from publicly disclosing their activities.

In seeking to justify, if not extend, its surveillance of suspected subversive activities, the Justice Department gave considerable publicity to the 1945 *Amerasia* case and the 1946 disclosure of a wartime Soviet atomic espionage ring in Canada. Both cases, they said, confirmed the existence of a potentially serious Soviet subversive threat—one which had to be met with far-reaching security measures. In making its plea, however, the Department failed to distinguish between the vastly different character of the two cases. The Canadian case was indeed espionage; the *Amerasia* case, in contrast, was more a political matter. The classified State Department documents on the administration's China policy which the editors of *Amerasia* (a radical journal concerned with Far Eastern affairs) had obtained surreptitiously from State Department personnel had, in fact, not been secured for the Soviet Union. The editors had simply used the documents to discredit the administration's protestations of neutrality in the Nationalist-Communist conflict and to support their own more radical China policy. This unauthorized use of classified information is not all that unusual in Washington; indeed, Washington correspondents have always depended upon internal departmental differences for information, classified or not, about the nature of administration policy.

Despite the obvious differences between the *Amerasia* and Canadian cases, the Justice Department succeeded in making both support a need for stricter surveillance of federal employees and American communists. This concern over communist "espionage" was fortified by fears about the role of communists in the flurry of labor strikes, racial incidents, and other radical activities that occurred in 1945–1946. Defending their actions in constitutional and civil libertarian terms, American communists were making political capital of the disparity between wartime rhetoric and domestic reality and the feelings of frustration within both the labor movement and the black community.

In response to these domestic developments, in July 1946 the Department of Justice urged President Truman to remove existing restrictions on its investigatory procedures; specifically, it asked for authorization for wiretapping. The President's consent was eventually obtained, but by highly questionable means. Attorney General Clark went about the job by carefully editing a 1940 Roosevelt directive in a way so as to foster the impression that Truman's approval was merely a reaffirmation of Roosevelt's action.* Although by this new directive the FBI was permitted to wiretap "subversive" and criminal persons, information so secured, owing to existent legislative and constitutional restrictions, was not admissible as evidence in court.

Along with obtaining the wiretapping authorization, the Justice Department also utilized a report from the Subcommittee of the House Committee on Civil Service recommending the establishment of a loyalty program to secure presidential consideration for a review of existing federal em-

---

* In 1940 Roosevelt had authorized his Attorney General, Robert Jackson, to resort to wiretapping in cases involving foreign espionage or sabotage. Seeking to limit the abuses of wiretapping, Roosevelt expressed his concurrence with Supreme Court decisions of 1939–1940 precluding the use of evidence gained by wiretapping, though he added that this restriction need not apply to national security cases. In 1946 Clark advised Truman of the 1940 directive and quoted from Roosevelt's final paragraph authorizing the FBI to wiretap in national security cases. Significantly, in quoting Roosevelt's directive, Clark did not include the last sentence of the paragraph, in which Roosevelt had distinctly limited the resort to wiretapping to cases clearly involving foreign espionage or sabotage and to aliens, not American citizens. This deletion, plus Clark's failure to report the gist of Roosevelt's reservations about wiretapping, enabled the Attorney General indirectly to secure Truman's assent to an extension of FBI wiretapping authority.

ployment procedures. The Roosevelt administration had established a limited security program during the war. But FBI investigations of federal employees, both before and during employment, had been restricted, and an employee could be dismissed only for overt acts of disloyalty or formal membership in the Communist party. In July 1946 Clark urged the President to establish a permanent loyalty program that would provide for the dismissal of an employee not only for overt actions but for "suspect" activities, associations, beliefs—anything that might confirm "potential" disloyalty.

While Truman was suspicious about communist activities, he was also hesitant to initiate a stringently restrictive loyalty program. Seeking to undercut this reservation on the President's part, Clark emphasized, first, the tighter security the new program would provide; and, second, the possible political disaster of inaction should the Republican congressional leadership independently review federal employment practices. Nonetheless, Truman hesitated to institute such a program, and merely instructed his White House staff to give the matter more study.

Political developments in 1946—chief among them, the election of a conservative Republican Congress and the rift over policy priorities between former Roosevelt New Dealers and Truman appointees which resulted in the resignations of Henry Wallace and Harold Ickes—ultimately led Truman to give in to Clark's request. In late November 1946 he thus appointed a Temporary Commission on Employee Loyalty to examine the effectiveness of existing federal employment procedures in protecting both national security and individual rights. He directed the Commission to report its findings by February 1, 1947, which was well before Congress could initiate its own program.

The haste with which this Commission review was instituted and completed—Truman had, after all, to beat the Republican Congress to the punch—practically ensured that the entire question of the need for a loyalty program would not be seriously explored. As might be expected, the Commission's conclusions were far from convincing. A March 21, 1947, memo (preceding by a day Truman's formal announcement of the loyalty program) from Budget Director James Webb to Attorney General Clark revealed the effect of this haste. Webb admitted:

> In the brief time available for analysis of this order, I am unable to evaluate fully its effect upon agency administration and upon appropriation requirements.* However, in view of the desire for immediate action, I can interpose no objection to the approval of the order.

The Commission's recommendations were implemented in the President's Executive Order 9835 of March 22, 1947. Federal agencies and departments were now given ultimate responsibility for initiating loyalty investigations, conducting loyalty hearings, and determining either clearance or dismissal of employees. Recognizing the suspicions of civil libertarians about the FBI, the Commission recommended that that agency be restricted to a functionary role in the program: its files and investigative services were to be made available to the various departmental loyalty officials, but the FBI itself was to play a passive role.

In reality, the vagueness of Truman's order on the administration of the program, and the pressures contributing to its establishment, finally insured that the Justice Department, and indirectly the FBI, would in fact have a dominant role. It was to be the Justice Department that determined loyalty standards, proscribed disloyal activities, and defined threats to national security. For one thing, Attorney General Clark was authorized to determine and list those organizations and activities which might confirm an employee's dis-

---

* This admission was a significant one: the formal nature of the program would depend on the establishment of both final authority and the source of funds.

loyalty. For another, the FBI's demand that the confidential nature of its sources be assured was adopted. Finally, the direction of any program shaped by FBI investigative reports made Justice Department-FBI dominance inevitable.

The ways that Clark and Hoover would influence the program had already been established in their testimony before the Temporary Commission. Concerned less with overt acts than an individual's potentiality for subversion, both men had urged the Commission to permit the FBI to refuse, if refusal was deemed advisable, to disclose its confidential sources. Warning against an undue emphasis on individual rights, Clark then proposed the establishment of a central board to review the loyalty decisions of the various agency boards. Clark further recommended that the FBI be delegated "continuing" responsibility to inquire into cases "involving alleged subversive activities on the part of incumbent Federal employees."

> The problem of subversive or disloyal persons in the Government is a most serious one. While the number of such persons has not as yet reached serious proportions, there is no doubt that the presence of any in the government service or the possibility of their entering are serious matters, and should cause the gravest concern to those charged with the responsibility of solving the problem. I do not believe that the gravity of the problem should be weighed in the light of numbers, but rather from the serious threat which even one disloyal person constitutes to the security of the Government of the United States.

Hoover was far more specific in outlining the nature of the threat of subversion:

> Subversive or disloyal persons constitute a threat to the Government of the United States by reason of their opportunity or ability to engage in any one or more of the following activities:
> a. Espionage on behalf of a foreign power or on behalf

of the subversive group or groups in which they have membership or with which they are sympathetic.

   b. Influencing the formation of policies of the United States either domestic or foreign so that these policies will either favor the foreign country of their ideological choice or will weaken the United States Government domestically or abroad to the ultimate advantage of the above indicated foreign power.

   c. Influencing the execution of the foreign or domestic policies of the United States Government or of the Federal agencies with which the employee is connected. . . .

   d. The spreading by the employee within his particular agency of the Federal service of propaganda favorable to the foreign country of his ideological choice in such a way as to influence other personnel of the agency and the expression of such propaganda to non-employees in such a way as to create an impression of official sanction to such propaganda.

   e. Recruiting of other individuals either fellow workers or non-Government employees for membership in the subversive or disloyal group which the employee represents.

Thus the Justice Department's goal in establishing the loyalty program was not simply the defensive one of combating espionage and sabotage, but was equally the offensive one of political surveillance. When, in response to Clark's arguments of political and budgetary efficiency, Truman instituted exclusive FBI jurisdiction over the loyalty program in May 1947, the original civil libertarian guarantees of the Temporary Commission were effectively canceled.

§🐦

   The next step in the Justice Department's takeover of the loyalty program was its restriction of outside access to the FBI loyalty files. The first formal restriction occurred when in December 1947 the Department of the Interior sought to obtain access to the files to ascertain the validity of disloyalty charges in order to permit an accused employee to prepare his defense.* The FBI's privilege of confidentiality triumphed, then and later: in March 1948 it was extended to congressional requests for departmental files.

The event that precipitated this later extension of the restriction to cover congressional requests was a subpoena from the House Committee on Un-American Activities for the complete investigative file of Edward Condon. Attorney General Clark did not want the loyalty files released to HUAC —or anyone else for that matter. The release (and public scrutiny) of the FBI reports would involve internal security in partisan politics, cut off possible sources of confidential information, and, by disclosing that the FBI investigations did focus on political reformers, provide documentation for liberal condemnations of FBI procedures and political orientation. Release of the reports to HUAC would, moreover, end the Justice Department's monopoly of internal-security matters and seriously damage its image of objectivity. In fact, release of these reports might result in requiring the FBI to provide conclusive evidence instead of mere suspicion to bring about an employee's dismissal.

Truman was induced to sign an Executive Order on March 14, 1948, which restricted congressional access to the loyalty reports by requiring that all requests for classified material be referred to the President for approval. He did so in fear that HUAC might use the reports either to develop investigative

---

* The original Executive Order establishing the loyalty program had permitted confidentiality "when essential to the protection of the informants or to the investigation of other cases. . . . Investigative agencies shall not use this discretion to decline to reveal such sources of information when such action is not essential." This qualification left open the issue of whether the imposition of confidentiality was to be exceptional and if the decision to restrict was to be the exclusive prerogative of investigative agencies. When pressed on this issue, Truman would uphold the exclusive prerogative of the FBI and the Department of Justice.

leads of its own or document charges that existing loyalty procedures were inadequate. Thus Truman had ostensibly assumed titular responsibility for the operation of the loyalty program; in reality, however, he had given the Justice Department and the FBI *carte blanche* in matters of internal security as well as a respectable cover under which to exercise it.

৯❧

CAPITALIZING ON the President's aversion to the 80th Congress and his mistrust of Soviet international actions and objectives, the Justice Department next pressed for administration approval of certain internal-security legislative proposals. These included making the unauthorized disclosure of "national defense" information a crime, giving the Attorney General the authority to order wiretapping in national-security cases, and extending the foreign-agent registration provisions to the Communist party and its alleged front organizations.

After having been submitted to the Bureau of the Budget for approval, these proposals encountered opposition from other departments, chief among them Treasury. On March 28, 1948, the Treasury Department recommended that the Budget Bureau insist that the language of the Justice draft be more specific on the matter of prevention of violations of civil liberties. In fact, Treasury proposed a number of amendments whose enactment would greatly have reduced the scope of the original bill. The Bureau of the Budget subsequently advised the Justice Department that it could present the bill to Congress as an executive proposal only if Treasury's suggestions were incorporated. By this time, however, Whittaker Chambers had made his dramatic presentation of the "Pumpkin Papers" in testimony before HUAC—an event that necessarily changed Justice Department strategy.

BEFORE Chambers' Pumpkin Papers testimony, and in part to win popular support for its legislative proposals, the Justice Department had been seeking simultaneously to quicken popular concern over internal security and to disparage HUAC's methods. Its disagreement with the Committee stemmed more from HUAC's Republican focus than from any principled objections to the Committee's efforts to alert the public to the seriousness of the communist menace. In many respects, the rhetoric of Justice Department spokesmen was as conspiratorial and overheated as that of individual members of HUAC. The Justice Department's objectives were dramatically advanced through a series of national addresses by Attorney General Clark. Emphasizing the grave threat that Soviet expansion in Europe posed to the United States, Clark linked these developments to internal security. Again and again he contrasted the godlessness and totalitarianism of communism to the Justice Department's vigilance; the "publicity-seeking, partisan[ism]" of congressional conservatives (symbolized by HUAC) to the Justice Department's disinterested objectivity.

Truman's stunning victory in the 1948 presidential campaign led him to support the Justice Department's attacks on HUAC. In post-election press conferences, Truman pointedly referred to the Committee as "defunct," obsolete, and unnecessary. To make his adjectives stick, he then directed the Attorney General to draft a resolution which the newly elected Democratic House leadership could use to amend House rules in order to terminate the Committee.

At this point, Whittaker Chambers produced his Pumpkin Papers and, apparently, confirmed his charges against Alger Hiss. Needless to say, any efforts to eliminate the Committee had themselves been eliminated. In the view of a majority of Americans, HUAC had proven its worth. The Justice De-

partment, unwilling to make Treasury's proposed amendments to its internal-security bill in the first place, and now
doubly unwilling in the face of an invigorated HUAC, requested presidential authorization to introduce its unamended
bill as a strictly departmental, as opposed to an administration, measure. In addition to its three original proposals—
making the unauthorized disclosure of national-defense
information a crime, giving the Attorney General the authority to order wiretapping in national-security cases, and
extending the foreign-agent registration provisions to the
Communist party and its various fronts—a new provision
called for the removal of the statute of limitations from
espionage cases. (This additional provision was intended to
deal with the fact that Alger Hiss under existing law in 1949
could be tried only for perjury, not for espionage.)

Although Truman did not formally authorize the Justice
Department to introduce the bill as an administration-
sponsored measure, neither did he prevent it from doing so.
Should Justice succeed in strengthening its methods of investigation and surveillance, it would deny HUAC—by then
one of Truman's most formidable as well as constant enemies
—further opportunities to exploit the internal-security issue.
But Truman was not yet ready to go all the way out on a limb
for the Justice Department. As things turned out, his failure
to do so had adverse political consequences for him. The
Justice Department's introduction of the bill made the Department seem a more careful watchman over national security than Truman. In fact, it gave the lie to Truman's continued
assurances that current security safeguards were adequate.

The administration was immediately confronted with this
problem when Mississippi's Senator James Eastland, chairman of the Judiciary Committee, invited White House representatives to testify on the Justice Department's proposed bill.
The White House declined the invitation, still wishing to avoid
taking any stand whatever on the bill. Moreover, it advised

the Justice Department to send its "lowest" member to testify, adding that whoever testified should simply explain the bill's provisions without advocating passage. More specifically, he should advise the Judiciary Committee: (1) that internal-security legislation was a matter of congressional decision; (2) that the Justice Department would not resist any Judiciary Committee amendment providing additional safeguards for civil liberties; and (3), if questioned, that the bill was strictly a departmental proposal which had not been authorized by the President.

The Justice Department effectively subverted each of these White House suggestions. It sent not its lowest but its highest member: Attorney General Clark himself appeared before the Judiciary Committee. In his testimony Clark concentrated on the first White House directive: that enactment of internal-security legislation was a congressional matter. The effect of his April 16, 1949, testimony, was revealingly reported by the *New York Times* as supporting the *"Administration's* anti-spying bill [italics added]," which was exactly the opposite of White House instructions. Clearly, the Justice Department was becoming increasingly independent of the White House.

᠍

CONTINUED Justice Department pressure for stronger internal-security legislation only increased congressional and popular doubts about the Truman administration. Why, after all, should Justice be so worried when the President continually affirmed that all was well? If Justice continued to propose legislative restrictions on individual liberties, it did not seem unreasonable to conclude that the situation had to be really serious. These proposals, moreover, were concurrent with both Justice Department and Loyalty Review Board pleas not merely to continue the loyalty program but to

amend the standard of dismissal from "reasonable grounds
. . . for the belief that the person involved is disloyal" to
"reasonable doubt as to the loyalty of the individual involved."

Along with being undertaken independently of White
House direction, the proposals were coupled with a renewed
speechmaking campaign on the part of Justice Department
spokesmen. Attorneys General Tom Clark and J. Howard
McGrath made special use of invitations from legal and professional groups to speak on the need for stronger legislation
to protect national security. Ostensibly defending administration procedures, both men praised the positive investigative
and prosecution record of their own Justice Department and
the FBI. The other side of this self-congratulatory gambit
was, naturally enough, warning the public against the communist threat. In this regard, Clark and McGrath emphasized
the need for new procedures—ones that in a "period of
emergency" and in the "interest of national survival" involved "temporary" restrictions on "normal" rights and
privileges.

According to Attorney General McGrath (who succeeded
Clark upon the latter's appointment to the Supreme Court in
August 1949), the communist threat was omnipresent. In an
April 19, 1950, address, he observed: "There are today many
Communists in America. They are everywhere—in factories,
offices, butcher shops, on street corners, in private business—
and each carries in himself the germs of death for society."

Communism was a force that threatened the religious and
political liberties of every American. "This Godless tyranny
of Communism," McGrath warned, "will always be a menace
to the internal security of the United States so long as Communist dictatorships menace the peace and security of the
world." He denied that a "good Communist could be a good
American." Above all, McGrath asserted, since communism
and Christianity had diametrically opposed objectives, com-

munism threatened the Church. Communists were required to do battle with all "God-fearing and freedom-loving men." And that, McGrath warned the public, "the Communist conspiracy—at this very moment—is endeavoring to accomplish. They are busy at work—undermining your Government, plotting to destroy the liberties of every citizen, and feverishly trying, in whatever they can, to aid the Soviet Union."

McGrath's rhetoric, particularly his failure to distinguish between communist ideology and actual espionage, his emphasis on the necessity for "temporary" restrictions on individual rights in this period of "emergency" and "national survival," significantly altered the framework within which the general public evaluated loyalty procedures. The force of this argument was unmistakable: if not only foreign spies but *any* man on the corner might be a communist working for the overthrow of America, and if in addition the survival of the nation was at stake, then the stricter security efforts advocated by the Justice Department must indeed be enacted as soon as possible.

FBI Director Hoover counseled similar vigilance. In a May 8, 1950, address, he argued that "tolerance for the lawless" should end. "Tolerance toward tyranny is absurd," he said. Although Hoover conceded that it might be difficult to determine subversion, he warned the nation against becoming unduly optimistic or lax because of the seemingly small number of communists: "In actual numbers, their membership may not be large, nor have the Communists polled at any time a large number of votes in an election. This has been cited by the ignorant and the apologists and the appeasers of Communism in our country in minimizing the danger of these subversives in our midst."

Undeniably, Hoover's and McGrath's rhetoric served to further the McCarthyite cause. The combination of Hoover's calls for an end to tolerance with McGrath's citation of the ubiquitousness of communists in American society coincided exactly with McCarthyite charges of the Truman administration's being "soft on communism." Only strict security legislation, vigilant investigation, and prosecution—all advocated in consort by the Justice Department, the FBI, and the McCarthyites in Congress—could contain and defeat the threat the communists posed. If in the process certain individual liberties fell by the wayside, their abrogation was justifiable in light of the ultimate victory of the "free world," for nothing less than national survival was at stake.

The effect on the Truman administration of this agreement between the Justice Department, the FBI, and the McCarthyites was twofold. First, it seriously undercut Truman's own efforts to subdue McCarthy and his supporters by praising his administration's record on internal security. Second, it led to a loss of public credibility for the President's policies. Truman's invocations of the Alien and Sedition Act of the 1790's, his citations of the guarantees of the Bill of Rights, and his attempt to minimize the communist threat by quoting the decline in membership and voting strength of the party—all now seemed naive and unrealistic in the light of HUAC revelations and the warnings of the Justice Department officials.

THE ADMINISTRATION did, however, temporarily regain some control over the Justice Department as the result of a debate in 1950 over an immigration bill. In 1949 Justice had supported an immigration bill that provided for the detention and indefinite imprisonment of aliens against whom warrants of deportation had been issued but whose native countries would not admit them. In 1950 the repressive features of this bill (H.R. 10), then under consideration by the House Judiciary Committee, led many liberal organizations, as well as the

White House staff, to oppose its passage. As a step in attempting to convince the Democratic leadership of Congress to oppose the bill, the White House staff urged President Truman to advise the Justice Department to drop its support of it. (Justice had earlier requested, and been denied, Budget clearance to introduce the measure as an administration-approved bill.)

By emphasizing the bill's repressive features, the White House staff, particularly Stephen Spingarn and Charles Murphy,* further sought to restrict Justice Department influence in the loyalty sphere. They thus urged the President to require the Department to review proposed internal-security bills on the basis of both internal security and individual civil liberties. Accepting Spingarn's and Murphy's recommendation, Truman directed the Justice Department not to support passage of H.R. 10.

The Justice Department ignored this presidential recommendation, however, and continued to seek congressional enactment of H.R. 10. Moreover, Justice's agitation for the bill created the impression that it was an administration measure. Apprised of this development, Spingarn informed Assistant Attorney General Peyton Ford that the President in fact remained opposed to H.R. 10. While expressing awareness of the President's position, Ford at the same time extolled the bill's merits. Were the President fully informed, Ford argued, he would surely change his mind.

Citing the Justice Department's unwillingness to cooperate with the administration, Spingarn and Murphy urged Truman to exercise more definite controls on the Department. Their efforts succeeded. After a May 18, 1950, meeting with his staff, Truman directed Attorney General McGrath to meet

*Murphy was legislative counsel to the President, Spingarn a presidential assistant with advisory responsibilities in the civil rights–civil liberties fields.

with Spingarn on May 19. The purpose of the meeting, the
President advised McGrath, would be to devise procedures to
insure that the Justice Department gave equal weight to internal security and individual liberties in formulating future
internal-security legislation. The upshot of that May 19
meeting was the establishment of a new legislative clearance
procedure whereby all Justice-proposed internal-security
measures, before they could be submitted either to the Bureau
of the Budget or Congress for consideration, would first have
to be reviewed by the Department of Justice's Civil Rights
section.

This White House pressure led the Justice Department to
reverse its official stance on the enactment of H.R. 10. In
response to a request from Congressman Adolph Sabath,
chairman of the Judiciary Committee, for the Justice Department's views on H.R. 10, Assistant Attorney General
Ford replied that the Department had consistently supported
legislation along the lines of the proposed bill; however, "in
view of certain recent decisions of the courts, the Department
is now giving further consideration to the whole problem
involving subversive and undesirable aliens."

THE OUTBREAK OF the Korean War put an end to any White
House efforts to restrain the zeal of the Justice Department.
Not only did Korea raise popular fears of a third world war,
it also sharpened popular anxieties about subversion. Legislative proposals to increase security safeguards became considerably more attractive to both the public and Congress.
Taking advantage of this changed political climate, Justice
acted to revive H.R. 10, its alien deportation bill. On July
17, 1950, presidential assistant Spingarn learned from the

Democratic House majority leader John McCormack that H.R. 10 had passed the House. When informed that Truman had opposed this bill, McCormack expressed surprise: representatives from the Department of Justice had told him that Truman *approved* the measure. Nor could Justice—or its bill—be stopped in the Senate. Public and congressional fears aroused by the Korean War insured the bill's passage. The President's earlier failure to restrict the Justice Department more fully had only increased Justice's desire to tighten internal security, as well as enhancing its ability to do so. As presidential assistant Richard Neustadt noted in a memo to Stephen Spingarn: "I have not checked with Justice [on their legislative priorities*] for fear that they would want to upgrade the priority of one or another of the internal security bills. (Congress will do enough of that on Justice's urging, if any, without White House intervention.)"

Indeed, following the outbreak of the Korean War, the Justice Department began to pressure Truman to release a statement establishing the FBI's central authority over national-security matters. On the recommendation of the National Security Council, which had also been considering the statement, Truman issued it on July 24, 1950. This was followed by a July 28 press release from Justice stressing the need for full public cooperation with the FBI:

> The forces which are most anxious to weaken our internal security are not always easy to identify. Communists have been trained in deceit and secretly work toward the day

*In July 1950 the White House staff had initiated a review of administration priorities as the result of the changed situation created by the Korean War. The staff had contacted the Departments of Defense, State, and Treasury, and the Bureau of the Budget and the National Security Resources Board to determine if they wished to upgrade earlier proposals or introduce new ones.

when they hope to replace our American way of life with a Communist dictatorship. They utilize cleverly camouflaged movements, such as some peace groups and civil rights organizations, to achieve their sinister purposes. While they as individuals are difficult to identify—the Communist Party line is clear. Its first concern is the advancement of Soviet Russia and the Godless Communist cause. It is important to learn to know the enemies of the American way of life.

This statement, given its particularly vágue but sweeping definition of subversion, widened the scope of public fears: now peace and civil rights activities, reformist movements, any group associated with advocating change, had become potentially subversive. Naturally enough, the Justice statement also strengthened support for the drastic restrictive and repressive measures introduced by Mundt, Nixon, Ferguson, Johnston, and McCarran which were then before the Congress.

As always, the White House staff opposed the McCarthyites in Congress. By the summer of 1950 Truman's staff was less confident that McCarthyite internal-security bills could be defeated simply on constitutional grounds. To defeat new legislation, the White House staff reversed its earlier opposition and now urged administration support for S. 595—the measure originally proposed by Justice in 1949. Simultaneously it urged the Justice Department to propagandize its proposal in order to insure congressional passage. (Specifically, S. 595 proposed that all communist and communist front organizations disclose their financial resources. The bill left the determination of "communist and communist front" to the Attorney General.)

Amounting to little more than a belated White House conversion to security legislation, this strategy merely enhanced Justice's leverage. Moreover, the statement drafted by Justice to justify the merits of its proposal indirectly strengthened the McCarthyite position. The main Justice argument for passing S. 595, after all, was that it presented "fewer constitutional questions" than the other (McCarthyite) bills under consideration.*

Throughout this critical period of congressional deliberation on the various legislative proposals, it was significant that Truman failed to provide resourceful leadership and, in contrast to the Justice Department, appeared more concerned over his public image than with the kinds of security measures that resulted. He responded to events rather than initiating them, and consistently failed to offer a necessary perspective on the legislation. This lack of leadership further reduced Truman's ability to control Justice's initiatives in the internal-security field. After 1950 and throughout 1951 Justice was thus able to advance legislation which even contradicted official White House policy. Insofar as the administration had already conceded for reasons of political expediency the necessity for additional internal-security legislation, whatever leverage it had once had to preclude enactment of legislation which contravened civil liberties was now greatly diminished. Indeed, its concern over safeguards for individual liberties appeared unrealistic in contrast to the Justice Department and the McCarthyites' more "realistic" approach to the communist threat.

Both Justice and the McCarthyites distinguished between the rights and privileges of loyal and disloyal citizens. Communists should not, they believed, enjoy the same rights as loyal Americans. In fact, during congressional delibera-

---

*Continuing its independent strategy, the Justice Department at this time drafted another bill for the use of Democratic Senate Majority Leader Scott Lucas amending the Foreign Agents Registration Act to require communist and communist front organizations to register as agents of the Soviet Union. The strategy behind this bill was also to divert popular attention from Republican-sponsored measures. Lucas was not told that the bill was Justice-originated; initially, he thought it had been prepared with White House approval.

tion on the McCarran bill, Justice pressed the federal courts
to deny any right to bail for the recently convicted Communist party leaders. Attorney General McGrath argued
that "the defendants have pursued and will continue to
pursue a course of conduct and activity dangerous to the
public welfare, safety and national security of the United
States." The revocation of bail to those who would abuse
constitutional safeguards, this reasoning went, was not itself
unconstitutional. Justice also proposed legislation to amend
Section 3141, Title 18 of the U.S. Code to empower the
courts to deny bail in all national-security cases. Bowing,
however, to White House opposition—hesitantly expressed,
though it was—Justice did agree in late 1950 to delay introducing the legislation until a soon-to-be-established presidential commission on internal security and individual rights
could review it.

Although the Justice Department's intentions may not
necessarily have run counter to White House policy, its
rhetoric certainly and consistently undermined it. Justice
sought passage of an alternative bill to the McCarthyite-
sponsored McCarran bill. It also drafted a statement for the
Democratic congressional leadership raising important constitutional and administrative objections to McCarran's omni-
bus proposal. The Department's formal militant stance,
however, made its opposition appear to be a matter of
political convenience rather than moral principle. While possibly unconstitutional, the McCarran bill was consistent with
Justice's overall objective of decisively containing the communist threat.

If Justice was correct about the serious nature of this
threat, then the excesses of the McCarran bill were probably
inevitable. Constitutional safeguards had been violated during earlier national crises; the situation in 1950 was not that
different. Moreover, once the McCarran Act was passed,
the Justice Department announced that it intended "vig-

orously" to enforce it. Although other executive departments supported Congressman Clarence Cannon's intention of drafting a bill that would repudiate the McCarran Act and amend other previous statutes to confine safeguards solely to national-security areas, Justice commendation of the Act never slackened.

ൠ

THROUGHOUT 1951 the Justice Department went on to demand the enactment of more internal-security legislation. It recommended that the statute of limitations not apply to national-security cases; that harsher penalties be provided for perjured testimony; that immunity from prosecution be granted to individuals whose testimony might be essential either to a grand jury or to congressional inquiry involving national security; that investigative agencies be permitted to wiretap in internal-security cases; and that conflicting testimony—as opposed to prosecution proof of untruth—be sufficient for a perjury conviction.

The unique nature of the internal-security threat, the Justice Department argued, necessitated these legislative changes. The "fanatical, well-trained and highly disciplined" nature of the communist movement, Attorney General McGrath avowed, required restrictions undreamed of fifteen years earlier. McGrath pointedly warned against permitting "those who seek to destroy our form of government . . . to escape detection and punishment" through safeguards guaranteed by the Bill of Rights:

> I wish to invite the attention of the Congress to a provision of law through which persons who may be guilty of criminal subversive conduct—or, indeed, of other crimes— have sometimes been able to frustrate our law enforcement officials and our courts, and remain at large with impunity to constitute an ever-present danger to society. This loophole

is the deliberate and malevolent abuse of the right to testify, on the ground of self-incrimination, before a grand jury, a court, or before an investigative body of the Congress.

Interpreted as protecting traitors and undermining security, civil liberties themselves suddenly came to represent a threat to the national interest. Although its intention may have been only to secure political support for its legislative recommendations and investigative procedures, the Justice Department's militantly anti-communist rhetoric and actions made possible an atmosphere in which McCarthyism could and did thrive.

7

Partisanship, Elitism, and the National Interest

DESPITE the assertion made by Democrats and Republicans that foreign policy questions properly transcended political differences, in postwar congressional debate and in the 1950 and 1952 election campaigns discussion of foreign policy was distinctly partisan. The foreign policy debate assumed its bitterest form during the McCarthyite-dominated period of 1950–1952. On the one hand, there was the frenzied self-righteousness of McCarthyite attacks on administration motives. On the other, there was the injured innocence of the administration, which came on repudiating McCarthyite charges as irresponsible, partisan, unfounded, and potentially harmful to the national interest. Both the administration and McCarthyites adopted a super-patriotic posture, each claiming they alone could save the nation from the communist hordes. The tone and character of this debate only served to confuse reality: in point of fact the self-interest of each side rarely coincided with the national interest.

Not that the debate had no important implications for American foreign policy; it did. In response to McCarthyite attacks on the loyalty of its personnel, the Truman administration became obsessed with establishing its anti-communist credentials. Thus it proceeded cautiously in policy decisions, for the most part avoiding anything that was potentially controversial. More concerned with discrediting the Truman administration than with offering realistic alternatives, McCarthy and his conservative congressional supporters capitalized on the belief in American omnipotence. Their main counterproposal to administration "weakness and vacillation" was to demand the repudiation of past policy decisions and policy-makers. To do so, they implied, would in itself insure United States victory in the Cold War. While no doubt emotionally and psychologically satisfying, in the final analysis the repudiation of past policy or policy-makers could hardly be expected to resolve specific crises. A policy of confrontation might alarm the Soviet Union and the NATO allies, but it would neither eliminate the Soviet Union as a major world power nor terminate communist control of Eastern Europe and China. The Cold War was not about to be won with grandiloquent speeches or empty threats.

In its opposition to the Truman administration, moreover, McCarthy and his followers revealed two inherent contradictions. Although the McCarthyites maintained that they were no more than disinterested patriots seeking to promote the national security, in fact their purposes remained basically partisan. In seeking the removal of security risks from the State Department, they hoped ultimately to discredit Truman to the extent that he could not be re-elected, and the Democratic party at large to the extent that it would suffer a major congressional defeat. Even more fundamentally, these congressional conservatives hoped to discredit all reform on the model of the New Deal. Over and above the security scare, they sought to bring about the election of a conservative Republican President and indeed a conservative reorientation of American politics generally.

These partisan—or, more precisely, conservative Republican—objectives dramatize the second contradiction of McCarthyism—its pseudo-democratic stance. Despite the fact that in the main the McCarthyites disdained the exercise of popular democracy in social and economic policy matters or as a theory of government—basically, they were responsive only to the business community—their critique of administration national-security policy demanded the restoration of "democratic" controls on executive power, an end to secrecy in government and to arbitrary unilateral executive action, and the restoration of the legislative branch to its proper role as repository of the popular will. Adamant supporters of loyalty oaths and surveillance of federal employees and controversial minorities, advocates of untrammeled congressional inquiry and a limited right to dissent, McCarthy and his supporters nonetheless chose to represent their authoritarian methods as having the democratic purpose of informing the public and safeguarding the rights of the majority.

These contradictions—between partisan objectives and a disinterested posture, between intolerance of dissent and the demand for an open debate on policy matters, between disdain for public controls over the private sector and a pseudo-democratic appeal to the public on national-security matters—constituted the substance of McCarthyism. Yet these contradictions are less revealing of McCarthyism than the post-war political climate in which it was able to flourish. By themselves the contradictions of McCarthyism should have sufficed to discredit the movement. Yet, during the 1950's, despite its attempts to defeat the McCarthyites' efforts, the Truman administration not merely failed to discredit McCarthyism, its efforts to do so actually reinforced it.

TRUMAN'S ASSESSMENT of Republican criticism was essentially that of a partisan Democrat who understood both policy and the office of the presidency not theoretically but on the basis of direct political experience alone. His years in the Senate had led him to consider Republican anti-communist attacks on the New Deal simply partisan ploys to divert public attention from an unpopular conservative domestic record. As President, he often relied on the advice of specialized assistants whose political orientation was frequently as intensely partisan as his own. Although Truman reserved the ultimate responsibility for all decision-making for himself, he remained quite heavily dependent on his assistants. Clearly, he never questioned their political biases—partly because he shared them, partly because he believed in their good faith and expertise, and partly because he preferred action to thought.

Truman's partisanship was particularly accentuated in the area of foreign policy. A politician rather than a statesman, Truman was more attuned to short-term requirements than long-run results. This predilection lent an *ad hoc* quality to his administration's decisions—decisions for which popular support could be gained only by rhetorical appeals. Truman deemed international politics too complex for the average citizen; only experts, he felt, could understand and properly respond to international developments. In fact, because he felt that mass public opinion was made up of limited understanding on the one hand and undue idealism on the other, he considered it as little more than a minor obstacle to carrying out his policies. Although democratic in his belief that political leaders should be responsive to the electorate, Truman was, operationally, an elitist who believed that a functioning democracy required reliance on the advice of disinterested specialists.

The administration's Soviet policy was a case in point. In all his efforts to contain the Soviet threat, Truman sought to do so without involving the nation in what might prove a divisive debate. In effect, this method necessitated formulating policy in a considerably less than open manner. As Truman viewed things, in both international and domestic politics, the NATO countries, Congress, and the public existed to ratify decisions, but not to take part in their formation.

In response to McCarthyite attacks, the administration justified its secrecy on the grounds of national security: openness, it was argued, would only result in a partisan debate that would undermine national unity and work to the benefit of the Soviet Union. In fact, Truman maintained, the McCarthyites themselves were only harming national unity by their attacks on administration policy. In the final analysis, then, the administration was asking the public uncritically to agree that secrecy in the formulation of policy was an absolute necessity, that there were no realistic alternatives to the administration's expertly devised policy decisions, and that administration critics could (it followed) be only short-sighted, misguided, or irresponsible.

§⤴

FROM 1946 through 1948, administration foreign policy was criticized from both the left and right. As fiscal conservatives, those congressional conservatives who preceded McCarthy assailed the administration's containment policy for what they believed to be its overextended international military and economic commitments. On the other end of the political spectrum, idealistic internationalists and political radicals, led by Henry Wallace, opposed the administration's reliance on military strength and instead demanded multilateralism— either by working through the United Nations or by minimizing conflict with the Soviet Union through accommodation and concession. The administration's internal-security policy decisions were similarly criticized by both McCarthyites and

Henry Wallace and his Progressive party. Whereas the McCarthyites questioned the administration's competence and sincerity in devising an adequate loyalty program, the Wallaceites feared that any loyalty program would ultimately undermine dissent, stifle political radicalism, and end in labeling all efforts at reform "subversive."

Because their base was congressional, the McCarthyites posed a more acute political problem for the Truman administration than did the Wallaceites. Through seniority, their command of congressional committee chairmanships enabled them either to propose or amend internal-security legislation or initiate searching investigations of administration policies and personnel.

Although the Wallaceites lacked this congressional base, they derived political power from their appeal to the liberal-radical constituency developed by Franklin Roosevelt and their ability to exploit liberal disaffection with Truman's foreign and domestic policy. In fact, they described themselves as the true successors and supporters of New Deal policies and principles.

Though they were a political minority, their base of support was nevertheless important to a Democratic victory. Their political strategy in the 1948 campaign was less a serious attempt to win the presidency for the Progressive party than to penalize the Democrats for supporting Truman's policies. While the more radical Wallaceites hoped to found a third national party, the principal aim of most Progressive party members was to dramatize traditional Democratic dependence on liberal-radical support by demonstrating the continued political strength of the urban New Deal coalition. They hoped to force the Democratic party's candidates and Platform Committee to commit themselves clearly to the causes of internationalism and civil liberties. Despite these efforts, however, the Wallaceites rather cynically accepted the prospect of Thomas Dewey's election on the premise that under Truman's leadership there was, and could be, no meaningful difference between Democratic and Republican policies.

❦

CONFRONTED WITH the political opposition of congressional conservatives and Wallaceites, Truman's 1948 campaign strategy was to exploit the extremism of both forces of opposition and to emphasize his own moderation. He posed the choice confronting the electorate in polar terms: his own administration's wise reformist centrism as against a rightist or leftist course of disastrous extremism. His rhetoric was intensely partisan, everywhere oversimplifying issues and distorting the positions of his opponents. His basic campaign theme was that a sound foreign policy which would bring about international peace depended upon a sound economy; and both peace and prosperity were attainable only if domestic and international problems were confronted wisely —which was to say, by the administration of Harry Truman.

Heavily emotional in rhetoric, the Truman campaign avoided discussion of both principles and policy; it neither established priorities nor delineated future administration proposals. Instead, Truman's rhetoric concentrated on the "hidden" motivations of administration critics. Either the McCarthyite or Wallaceite approach, Truman said, would bring about disaster in the form of a depression, a world war, or a communist international victory and consequent takeover of the United States.

Administration spokesmen represented Wallace and the Progressives as advocates of "peace at any price" and ultimately as "appeasers." Wallace and his followers, these spokesmen maintained, were actually seeking to advance Soviet interests—a charge they supported by citing the

Wallaceites' double-standard of protesting United States foreign policy but remaining silent over Soviet policy in Eastern and Central Europe. In fact, the President and his spokesmen went on to claim, the Wallaceites' main support came from "Communists, Communist travelers and reactionary Republicans." Communist participation in the Wallace candidacy only confirmed communist influence in, if not control of, the Progressive party. According to Democratic National Committee Chairman J. Howard McGrath, the Progressive party's support derived from those "whose basic allegiance is not to the American way of life." McGrath added that the Wallace campaign was simply "the old Communist tactic carried forward with catchwords, catch phrases, trick tunes and stage-managed effects. Their one objective has been to aid the program of Russia."

Truman himself openly denounced the support of "Wallace and his Communists." "Communists are guiding and using the third party," he said. Peace, he argued, could not be won by blind hopes or trust but only by a policy of strength and resolve. Since existing international problems stemmed directly from a policy of accommodation and negotiation, Wallace-style "appeasement" would only result in the advancement of Soviet influence, if not in world war—and, for America, an unwinnable war at that.

Truman also raised the internal subversion issue to defend his own administration's loyalty program while simultaneously discrediting the loyalty of Wallace and the Progressive party. The federal government, Truman argued, had the responsibility to defend itself and the public from individuals who sought to use political freedom to subvert liberty and aid the interests of other countries. The threat was not a minor one, however it might appear to be, but potentially very serious indeed. The Democratic party had acted boldly to minimize this threat, and was not about to be lulled to sleep by vague appeals to liberty and freedom. These themes were dramatically expressed in a Democratic National Committee press release supporting Hubert Humphrey's candidacy for the Senate:

> The Democratic Party owes an unusual debt of gratitude to Mayor Hubert Humphrey. In fact, all the people of America are indebted to him.
> In no other state was an established political party in danger of being captured by Kremlin agents in order to disguise their political activity under a cloak of American respectability. If they had been successful in Minnesota, they would have extended their techniques to other states.

A second thrust of Truman's campaign strategy was to identify the Progressive party campaign with Republican reactionism. Referring to the "Wallace-GOP coalition," Truman charged that support for the Progressive party would indirectly strengthen conservative Republicanism. The basis of this argument, an argument by which Truman hoped to win back disaffected liberals, was that the Wallaceite "appeasement" approach to foreign policy would encourage international Soviet aggression; and that, moreover, the Progressive party's disruption of the two-party system would redound primarily to the conservatives' domestic advantage, with the overall effect being irreparable damage to American liberalism. By frightening liberals about the possible consequences of a Republican victory, the administration hoped to gain their support for Truman's candidacy quite independently of his administration's past record.

In his campaign opposition to the congressional conservatives, Truman affirmed that his administration had initiated positive and effective means for confronting both Soviet international expansion and internal subversion. As for Soviet expansionism, Truman said, policies such as the Truman Doctrine, the Marshall Plan, the Berlin airlift, the diplomatic nonrecognition of communist countries in Eastern Europe, and the support of South Korea and Nationalist China confirmed the administration's effectiveness in checking the Soviet threat. The continuation of these programs, Truman added, would result in the United States successfully forcing the Soviet Union to conclude a meaningful accommodation.

The 1948 Democratic party platform announced Truman's attitude toward internal-security matters: "We shall continue to build firm defenses against communism by strengthening the economic and social structure of our country. We reiterate our pledge to expose and prosecute treasonable activities of anti-democratic and un-American organizations." Truman himself felt that his administration had successfully protected the national security. In innumerable speeches he cited the establishment of a federal employee loyalty program (one that provided safeguards for both internal security and individual liberties), the prosecution of Communist party leaders, continued executive efforts to avert potential cases of sabotage and espionage, and statistics detailing the decline in voting strength and membership of the American Communist party since the adoption of the New Deal as proof of his administration's vigilance. As further evidence of his sound anti-communist credentials, both Truman and the Democratic National Committee stressed the Soviet Union's bitter opposition to administration foreign policy, as well as the American Communist party's equally bitter attacks on administration internal-security policy. On the offensive, Truman questioned the motivations behind Republican efforts to raise the loyalty issue. Their objectives were two, he charged: to evict Democrats, not communists, from Washington; and to divert public attention from the "reactionary" record of the 80th Congress.

Seeking to impugn the congressional conservatives—who were themselves impugning his administration's insufficient anti-communism—Truman and his spokesmen described the

Republican leadership of the 80th Congress as partisan and isolationist. Their opposition to such internationalist policies and institutions as the United Nations, the Truman Doctrine, and Marshall Plan, it was argued, had crippled administration efforts to protect the national interest. Had conservative opposition ever led to the defeat of any of these policies, the cause of Soviet expansion would have been advanced. Ultimately, Truman and his spokesmen charged, the result would have been world war in extremely disadvantageous circumstances for the United States. In support of this contention, Democratic National Chairman McGrath described isolationist Republicans as a "fearful echo of that other Republican isolationist group that denied active American participation and support for the League of Nations and paved the way for a Second World War."

McGrath's comparison exemplified a basic element in the administration's campaign strategy. Relying on the popular belief that interwar isolationism had made World War II possible, the Democrats continually identified conservative "partisan" and "isolationist" efforts to block or restrict international aid programs with the Republican role in the 1919 Senate rejection of United States involvement in the League of Nations.

The administration further sought to discredit conservative Republicanism by implying that the domestic policies of the 80th Congress were harming the national security. Had not the isolationist and protectionist policies of conservative Republicans in the 1920's led to the American depression and a world economic crisis? Of course they had, Truman said, thus emphasizing that only a sound, progressive economy could provide the resources, both economic and military, that an advanced international power required. Since communism always exploited misery, poverty, and discontent, any effective countersubversive policy had to have at its base a sound domestic economy.

§➋

IT WAS IN Truman's dealings with the House Un-American Activities Committee, however, that he really came to grips with McCarthyism. Contrasting the restraint and procedural correctness of his administration's loyalty program to HUAC's record of unsubstantiated charges and hearsay testimony, he dismissed the Committee's charges as the effect of a combination of partisanship and simple publicity-seeking. The Committee's tactics in 1948—its overt hostility to the New Deal, its quest for publicity, and its abuse of individual rights—all tended to confirm Truman's criticism. It was not so much that the public believed Truman to be nonpartisan, but rather that it found the Committee irresponsibly so.

Indeed, the Committee's investigations at the time concentrated less on acts of overt disloyalty than on private beliefs and associations. It was this that enabled Truman successfully to assail HUAC on civil libertarian grounds. That the administration itself had, under cover of executive privilege, resorted to censorship, restricted congressional access to loyalty reports, and attempted to preclude an independent congressional investigation of its loyalty program did not then seem to many Americans to usurp legislative prerogatives or constitute an unwarranted executive assumption of power. Truman easily justified these actions as the proper democratic response to HUAC's distortions. The seeming success of his administration's foreign and internal-security policies further supported Truman's claims: by 1948 there had been no serious incident involving either foreign policy failure or individual disloyalty.

These same administration tactics had become untenable by 1950. The damning evidence of federal employee disloyalty produced by the Pumpkin Papers, Soviet explosion of an atomic bomb, and the defeat of the Chinese Nationalists created doubts about the Truman administration's diplomatic and security policies as well as its personnel. The administration, however, changed neither its 1948 campaign tactics nor its rhetoric to fit this new political atmosphere. Its failure to appreciate that its earlier successes against congressional conservatives had derived from the uniqueness of conditions during 1946–1948 seriously undermined its credibility in 1950. The demise of the Progressive party had by 1950 removed what, during 1946–1948, had been an effective counter-balance to the conservatives, thereby leaving the comfortable middleground position to Truman. The administration could no longer capitalize on Wallace-like denunciations claiming that its policies were reactionary to assume the moderate posture of balancing safeguards against subversion with safeguards for the civil liberties of individuals.

BY 1950 popular concern had shifted from economic issues and concern over conservatism to national security and fear of radicalism, from suspicions about the objectives of the 80th Congress to a loss of faith in the Truman administration. This change in national politics was directly related to the change in character of the Chambers-Hiss confrontation. In early 1948 the focus of Chambers' charges had been anti–New Deal. Testifying before HUAC he had accused Hiss only of being a member of the Communist party, whose function had been to promote communist infiltration of the New Deal. In response, in August 1948, Truman could disparage this testimony as simply a "red herring," an unsubstantiated result of partisan publicity-seeking. Moreover, Truman was also able to mute the impact of Chambers' charges and simultaneously establish his own anti-communist stance by initiating a Justice Department investigation.

By immediately adopting this posture, instead of questioning whether Hiss's activities were in fact treasonable, Truman emerged as more anti-communist than HUAC itself. His implicit acceptance of the notion that membership in the Communist party equalled treason served to legitimize the investigation of the past activities of all federal employees. In early 1948 neither Truman nor HUAC distinguished between simple Communist party membership and the intent to commit treason. Truman's defense of individual liberties centered on the loyal and unfairly accused; he thus implicitly accepted the need to deal vigorously with the "disloyal."

Once Chambers produced the Pumpkin Papers in December 1948, however, Truman's and HUAC's public credibility standings were significantly reversed. Chambers' testimony confirmed his own subversive activities. If it could also be proved that Chambers, an admitted former communist, had received these confidential State Department documents from Hiss, then HUAC's demand for improvements in federal loyalty procedures and its identification of radicalism with treason would be greatly enhanced. Moreover, Truman's earlier charge against the Committee's partisanship would seem very pale indeed.

Truman did not, however, change his tack. In fact, he responded to the December disclosure by defensively reiterating his earlier "red herring" charge. Once again the administration sought to impugn the Committee's motives by self-righteously adopting the position of "true" spokesman for the people. A December 10, 1948, statement released by Democratic National Chairman J. Howard McGrath made this plain:

> One of the greatest problems in an election year when a congress is repudiated by the voters is the interregnum between the election date and the date on which the new Congress takes office. . . .
> This bridge period, between November 2 and January 3, is particularly difficult when defeated members of Congress

fail to realize that no longer do they speak for the People. . . .

Repudiated and discredited in the handling of the House Un-American Activities Committee, for instance, key Republicans are still talking and making gestures against the Administration and the Federal Grand Jury system that fit the political gesturing and talking in which they indulged prior to November. . . .

At the very moment that the Federal Grand Jury is acting against spies and spy rings the committee is racing to milk the situation of its last headline and the final newsreel and radio shot.

They have withheld information from the Attorney General. They have done everything to cripple legal, proper investigation and they do all this in a highly political atmosphere.

The implication that any independent congressional investigation necessarily had to be partisan—and, by extension, irresponsible—was the Truman administration's formal response to the McCarthyites.* Given the circumstances created by HUAC's uncovering of the Pumpkin Papers, McGrath's reference to "withholding" of information and "crippling" investigations appeared as a pale partisan effort to immobilize the Committee and thus avoid an independent examination of executive loyalty procedures. The heavyhandedness of the administration's posture of expertise and its demand for uncritical acceptance of exclusive executive control was politically washed out in light of Chambers' disclosures. Obviously, the American public concluded, the administration's security procedures had broken down, which made it seem that only an independent—even a partisan—congressional committee

---

*Indeed, Truman periodically resorted to this tactic in 1949 and 1950 when responding to McCarthyite charges. In 1949 he would dismiss HUAC allegations of a security threat as an attempt to secure headlines; in 1950 he would describe McCarthy as "the best asset the Kremlin has," because his attacks on State Department personnel harmed bipartisanship in foreign policy and thereby benefited Soviet interests.

could provide the necessary safeguards against future administration errors. In disparaging HUAC methods, the administration had missed the real point: no matter *how* the discovery had been made, Chambers' testimony revealed that national security was indeed endangered.

HAVING ASSUMED the role of unquestioned (and unquestionable) expert in national-security matters, the administration then affirmed that its own resort to secrecy in the operation of the loyalty program and the conduct of foreign relations was essential to the national interest. Specifically, it refused to permit congressional access to federal employee loyalty files, exempted the CIA from the obligation to disclose either the names of its employees or the uses of its appropriated funds, clamped shut the lid on the atomic energy program, delayed publication of the Yalta agreements and proceedings, and refused to release the Wedemeyer Report on China.* Concurrently, Truman charged those Congressmen demanding publication of policy decisions with irresponsibly endangering the national interest for selfish partisan purposes. And, finally, Truman continued to refuse to cooperate with HUAC.

In response to McCarthy's communists-in-the-State-Department charges, the administration threw its support to the investigations of a special subcommittee of the Senate Foreign Relations Committee chaired by Millard Tydings (Democrat, Maryland). The Democrats in the Senate had initiated what became known as the Tydings investigation

---

*These actions provided a new basis for conservative attacks on executive authority. Indeed, in his February 20, 1950, Senate speech, when he affirmed that he had evidence confirming the existence of eighty-one "Communists in the State Department," Senator McCarthy prefaced his remarks by emphasizing that he had penetrated "Truman's iron curtain of secrecy."

mainly to discredit McCarthy by proving that his charges had no basis in fact. Thus Tydings initially confined the scope of his inquiry to the specific eighty-one cited cases of State Department disloyalty that McCarthy had presented to the subcommittee.

While the McCarthyites immediately charged that the inquiry was a cursory one designed to "whitewash" the State Department, the real bombshell came when Tydings requested presidential authorization to examine the confidential loyalty files of the eighty-one "defendants." In order to grant the request, Truman would have to reverse his earlier (March 1948) Executive Order denying congressional committees access to the loyalty files, and in the bargain possibly establish an embarrassing precedent.

Simultaneously pressed by the Justice Department and the FBI not to revise his 1948 order and by the State Department to provide the subcommittee full access to the files, Truman eventually acceded to Justice and denied the subcommittee's request. Once again he justified his decision on the grounds of national security—specifically, that disclosure of FBI sources might cut off further information. Concurrently, however, he urged all federal departments, particularly the State Department, to cooperate fully with the subcommittee. To ensure that the subcommittee received maximum information, Truman directed the Loyalty Review Board to study the files of the eighty-one cases and report its findings to him. The board, Truman claimed, would have unrestricted access to all information developed by the FBI, the State Department, and the civil service.

Senator McCarthy and his supporters denounced this administration decision, arguing that the subcommittee, and not an executive-appointed board which had already failed in its responsibilities, could best provide a meaningful review of the cases. In a telegram to Truman, McCarthy demanded that the President accede to the subcommittee subpoena for the files, adding that "I feel that your delay of the investigation by your arrogant refusal to release all the necessary files is inexcusable and is endangering the security of the Nation."

Taking the offensive, the McCarthyites went on to accuse Truman of attempting to "smear" McCarthy and other critics of his administration's foreign policy for the purpose of preventing a needed investigation. They particularly assailed Truman's March 30, 1950, press conference remarks identifying McCarthy as "the best asset the Kremlin has" and his public statements in April contending that criticisms of his administration's foreign policy were efforts to "sabotage the foreign policy of the United States [which] is just as bad in this cold war as it would be to shoot our soldiers in the back in a hot war."

The McCarthyites further contended that the President's restriction on the subcommittee's access to the loyalty files was simply an attempt to cover up executive error. In support of McCarthy, Senator Robert Taft urged the Senator to persist: "if one case doesn't work . . . bring up others." Praising the "fighting marine [McCarthy] who risked his life to preserve the liberties of the United States," and assailing Truman's refusal to allow "any representative of Congress" to review the loyalty files, Taft asked, "What is he [Truman] afraid of?" He decried the President's efforts to "condemn any Republican who disagrees with Mr. Truman's unilateral foreign policy secretly initiated and put into effect without any real consultation with Congress." Taft then noted of the President's loyalty program that "the facts already proved about Hiss . . . in the State Department justify our support of an investigation unhampered by executive obstinacy and name-calling."

In the end, Truman succumbed to McCarthyite pressure and authorized the Tydings Committee to investigate the State Department loyalty records. He still excluded access to FBI files, however. Tydings stated that he personally would conduct the investigation of the State Department records. McCarthy immediately attacked both Truman's limited authorization and Tydings' personal review; only the Tydings Committee's staff investigators, he claimed, had the expertise to determine how badly the files might have been "rifled." Once Tydings' report was published, McCarthy dismissed the findings as incomplete and censored. The Tydings report, he said, did not include even all the evidence that he had presented to the subcommittee in his own report, thereby confirming the extent to which the files had been "raped."

Throughout the debate over access to the loyalty files—up to and including publication of the Tydings report—Truman had given McCarthy an excellent opportunity to publicize his claims of the administration's laxity and indifference on matters of security. Both in defending confidentiality and in subsequently loosening restrictions on the Tydings investigation, Truman failed to resolve the deep popular doubts about existing security procedures that McCarthy and his congressional supporters had raised. Nor did the President once rise above the McCarthyites to address himself to such real issues as: what is the definition of disloyalty, when and under what conditions can restrictions on individual liberties and due process be justified, and what was the true nature of the information sources in the FBI loyalty reports?

THE RHETORIC that Truman and the Democratic National Committee adopted during the 1950 congressional campaign further increased popular doubts about administration priorities. At the same time Truman admitted the gravity of the communist threat and defended his administration's efforts to contain it, he emphasized the bipartisan character of his national-security policies. Many Republicans held important posts in the State Department, he pointed out, and a Republican was chairman of the Loyalty Review Board. Thus, he contended, Republican (i.e., McCarthyite) criticism of his policies was essentially isolationist, irresponsible, publicity-seeking, and, by undermining national unity, both harmful to United States' interest and beneficial to the communists.

Similarly, the Democratic National Committee urged local, state, and congressional candidates to concentrate on Republican opposition (in the House vote of January 1950) to the Korean Aid bill. The Democratic leadership worked over-time against Senator Taft's re-election campaign. Taft's op-position in 1947 and 1948 to containment measures proposed by the President and adopted by Congress, it was charged, had indirectly aided the Soviet Union. Taft's early isolationism was also blamed for contributing to the expansion of Hitler's Germany in the 1930's and Stalin's Russia in the 1940's.

Such rhetoric contained inherent contradictions that were politically disastrous. The appointment of a few Republicans to policy positions in the State Department hardly indicated true bipartisanship; and in fact the real authority and re-sponsibility for foreign policy continued to reside with Demo-crats. In essence, the Democrats confirmed the McCarthyite charge that the Truman administration had used its "bi-partisan" foreign policy to partisan advantage by silencing Republican criticism, dividing the Republican party, and sub-verting its surveillance through limited participation in decision-making.

When the administration tried to malign McCarthyism, it only did further damage to its own image. Despite their formal pronouncements on McCarthy's ineffectiveness, both the administration and the Democratic National Committee were indeed seriously worried about the Senator's overall im-pact. In contrast to Truman's confident assertion, after return-ing from a trip through the West in late spring 1950, that McCarthy did not appear to have any popular following, be-hind the scenes the Democratic National Committee and administration spokesmen were drafting a special study for the use of sympathetic Senators detailing replies to McCarthy's various charges. At the same time the Democratic National Committee published a series of interviews with FBI Director Hoover and Attorney General McGrath extolling the virtues of the Truman administration in handling the grave communist threat. Hoover and McGrath also stressed the need to keep the loyalty files confidential at the same time that they urged greater public defense against communist subversion.

Silence, indifference, direct and indirect rebuttal—all these ploys failed to undercut the thrust of McCarthyism. At first it appeared that it was only pride which prevented the administration's considering McCarthy's accusations. Then the form of the administration's responses—making changes in established internal-security legislation and rulings on congressional access to the loyalty reports while claiming that everything was in order—provided seeming confirmation for the McCarthyite contention that change was indeed required.

Moreover, the Democratic leadership's own red-baiting did not differ substantively from McCarthyite tactics. In 1950, for example, the Democratic State Central Committee of Pennsylvania published a pamphlet entitled "Fellow Traveling Pa. GOP Congressmen Follow Red Party Line." In that pamphlet the committee compared the foreign policy voting records of Pennsylvania Republican Congressmen with that of the leftist New York Congressman Vito Marcantonio. Strikingly similar to Richard Nixon's famous "pink sheet," this line of attack was recommended for the use of local and national Democratic candidates by men within both the administration and the Democratic National Committee.

§❧

STILL REFUSING to change his approach, still hoping to discredit McCarthy's charges, in January 1951 the President appointed a special commission on internal security and individual rights. He directed the commission to examine existing loyalty procedures in the light of possible abuses of individual liberties as well as their effectiveness in averting subversion, and to recommend whether additional legislation or changes in the loyalty program were needed. The idea of a commission study of the loyalty program had been suggested from time to time since 1948 by many liberals. Truman, however, did not act upon their suggestion until the impact of McCarthyism had been dramatized by the enactment of the McCarran Act and the strong McCarthyite showing in the 1950 congressional elections. When he did act, his principal purpose was to defend the existing loyalty program and not, as the objective of the earlier proposals implied, to minimize the program's infringement of individual civil liberties. The commission was to be blue-ribbon and nonpartisan, composed of respected people outside of government. Truman first asked Herbert Hoover to accept the chairmanship. An acknowledged anti-communist, Hoover had the political advantage of being a conservative Republican who was not especially identified with civil libertarianism. While his chairmanship of the commission would not ensure that abuses to individual rights would be corrected, it would disarm any McCarthyite attack on the commission's recommendations by giving the commission an independent and nonpartisan character.

Hoover, however, turned down the President's request. A presidentially appointed commission was not, Hoover wrote Truman, the best way to restore public confidence in the government's conduct of foreign relations. That loss of confidence, he said, stemmed not from concern over libertarian abuse but from mistrust of certain individuals who continued to make foreign policy. Conceding that these individuals were not card-carrying Communists, Hoover went on to argue that their attitudes were nevertheless "such that they have disastrously advised [the President] on policies in relation to Communist Russia." Instead of a presidential commission, Hoover contended, it was Congress who should investigate not only existing loyalty procedures but, more importantly, the past and present activities of federal employees. Essential to such an investigation, he said, was the right of congressional access to all loyalty files. Hoover concluded by urging Truman to recommend the establishment of such a congressionally created commission. Not surprisingly, Truman disregarded all of Hoover's recommendations.

Eventually Truman persuaded former Admiral Chester Nimitz to serve as chairman, and established the commission by a presidential Executive Order in which he ceded full investigative powers, including access to confidential loyalty files, to its members. The McCarthyites immediately attacked both the presidential establishment of the commission and its investigative prerogatives. Both features of the commission, they charged, confirmed Truman's hostility toward Congress and his desire to whitewash the administration's loyalty record. Only Congress, they claimed, had both the independence and investigative power to provide the necessary impartial review of existing executive loyalty procedures.

The McCarthyite critique was well-founded. By disdaining congressional involvement, Truman was still seeking to establish the administration's absolute expertise in loyalty matters. He resolutely believed that existing procedures were basically correct and McCarthyite charges basically irresponsible. Moreover, he continued to claim the necessity for confidential nature of information on civil libertarian and national-security grounds.

For all these reasons, Truman's commission failed to resolve popular doubts about the adequacy of existing safeguards against internal subversion. In fact, the appointment of the commission only intensified these doubts by appearing to be a tacit presidential admission that existing procedures were inadequate. These doubts were then exacerbated by the administration's April 1951 decision to amend the standard for dismissal on loyalty grounds.

The Loyalty Review Board and the Justice Department, both extremely security-conscious, had been urging Truman to amend the dismissal standard since 1949. Their main argument was that the original requirement of conclusive proof of disloyalty had enabled "potentially" disloyal individuals to secure a loyalty clearance. Accordingly, the board had recommended amending the dismissal standard to "reasonable doubt" of the individual's "loyalty." Because this proposal subordinated individual liberties to administrative considerations, it had been successfully opposed on civil libertarian grounds by other federal agencies as well as by individual members of the White House staff. By 1951, however, the administration's desire to quell popular doubts about the loyalty of federal personnel at any cost had become primary.

Thus in April the President issued an Executive Order establishing the new standard for dismissal. Immediately thereafter, the board instituted a review of all earlier cases wherein individuals had been cleared on appeal. The most notable case of an individual cleared under the old standard and dismissed under the new was that of Foreign Service officer John Stewart Service.

For many McCarthyites, Service, as we have noted earlier, had long symbolized the laxity of administration loyalty procedures. A Far East expert during the 1940's and an outspoken critic of the Nationalist Chinese, he had recommended a policy of neutrality in the civil conflict between the Chinese Communists and Nationalists. Both this recommendation and Service's wartime associations with Philip Jaffe, editor of *Amerasia,* had contributed to doubts about his loyalty. Yet before 1951, although subjected to six loyalty-security checks and three loyalty hearings, Service had been cleared both on loyalty and security grounds. In 1951, however, under the new standard, the Loyalty Review Board found that Service's independent declassification of certain documents found in the June 1945 FBI raid of the *Amerasia* offices raised doubts about his loyalty. Although the board absolved Service of communist sympathies, it recommended his dismissal. Secretary of State Dean Acheson affirmed this decision.*

Far from benefiting the administration, both the changed standard and Service's dismissal only heightened the seeming inadequacy of former loyalty procedures. The timing of the revision of the dismissal standard made it appear that it was pressure exerted by the McCarthyites, and not any administration soul-searching, that had led it to act. Thus a change instituted to undercut McCarthyism in effect served to legitimize it.

THROUGHOUT 1951, Truman sought to preserve presidential prerogatives from congressional encroachment. This goal was nowhere more apparent than in his dispatch of troops to Korea. A President, Truman argued, had the right to send American troops anywhere in the world without a congressional declaration of war. While he did say he would consult and inform Congress in particular situations, he still contended that the need for immediate action and secrecy might at times require unilateral presidential action.

Widening still further the traditional executive-legislative

---

*When Service brought a court suit against the State Department seeking the reversal of this decision, the dismissal was reversed in 1957 on technical grounds and the Department was ordered to reinstate Service. Yet this court decision did not undo the damage to Service's career, nor did it offset the popular impact of the 1951 dismissal—affirming as it did a consistent McCarthyite contention.

conflict, Truman then suggested that the President alone had the information and means necessary to make sound policy. Congress did not know enough to make the reasoned judgments the President could, nor was it sufficiently flexible to act as quickly as the President often had to. Welcoming the confrontation with Congress that these views produced, Truman declared that he had "licked" a recalcitrant Congress in 1948, and that he was ready to go the people again should Congress not accept his views.

Precisely this sort of attitude made Truman seem obsessed with power. His challenge to Congress and his justifications of presidential secrecy, which threatened to undermine the traditional restraints on executive authority embodied in the checks and balances of the Constitution, enabled McCarthy and his conservative congressional supporters to adopt the stance of supporting "democratic" controls (limited government) and congressional prerogatives. Since Congress traditionally had exclusive authority to declare war and conduct investigative hearings, the McCarthyites had gained an obvious rhetorical advantage over Truman.

What Truman overlooked in his challenge to Congress was that the powers of a President are not based simply on constitutional provisions but on the degree of his political strength as well. During the 1940's, because of popular confidence in the President and widespread antipathy toward Congress, Roosevelt had been able to extend executive authority in matters of foreign policy. By 1951, however, the situation had been drastically reversed. Now the public trusted Congress while it doubted Truman's abilities and purposes.

Long-simmering congressional ill-feeling brought about by United States involvement in Korea, which Congress had resented but hesitated to overturn, came to a head with Truman's announcement that four American divisions would be assigned to support NATO in Europe. Truman's NATO decision corresponded roughly to his earlier Korean commitment in that the presence of American troops in both Europe and Asia could lead to war independent of a congressional declaration. But because the European situation (in contrast to that in Korea) did not require an immediate military response, Congress forced Truman to secure its approval of the NATO commitment. The subsequent Senate debate centered not on the deployment of American troops in Europe but on the questions of the President's right to assign troops overseas and Congress' exclusive authority to declare war. While these two conflicting prerogatives provided the formal basis for the debate, what was really on review was President Truman's credibility.

The debate began with Senator Kenneth Wherry (Republican, Nebraska), an outspoken McCarthyite, introducing a resolution in the Senate to prohibit the assignment of United States ground troops to NATO without congressional approval. Wherry's resolution failed to pass, and the Senate subsequently approved a pro-administration resolution, S. Res. 99, introduced jointly by Senators Tom Connally (Democrat, Texas) and Richard Russell (Democrat, Georgia) on behalf of the Committees on Foreign Relations and Armed Services. Nonetheless, the clamor raised by the McCarthyites over Wherry's resolution forced administration supporters to amend the Connally-Russell resolution.* The amended version specified that only four divisions were to be

*The most important amendment to S. Res. 99 was introduced by Senator John McClellan (Democrat, Arkansas). His intent was to approve the assignment of the four divisions but establish Congress' future authority. Thus, whereas the original Connally-Russell resolution had stipulated that congressional approval "should be obtained of any policy requiring the assignment of American troops abroad," McClellan's amendment clearly specified: "but it is the sense of the Senate that no ground troops in addition to such four divisions be sent to Western Europe in implementation of article 3 of the North Atlantic Treaty without further congressional approval."

assigned to Europe; should additional ones be required, the President would first have to secure the assent of Congress. The resolution also stated that Congress had not renounced its exclusive power to declare war.

Despite the accommodations inserted into S. Res. 99, the President reaffirmed his constitutional right as commander-in-chief to assign troops overseas, even in the absence of congressional approval. To support his claim, Truman cited both the gravity of the Soviet threat and the possible need for an immediate military response, brought about by the development of atomic weapons. Effective action in either case, he argued, could only be provided by unrestrained executive authority.

Although in this instance Truman had secured congressional approval for his decision to deploy troops in Western Europe, the approval in no way reflected support of his leadership or of his claims to authority. Both congressional and popular acceptance of the troop deployment were predicated on simple fear of Soviet objectives. Thus the troop deployment was regarded as a deterrent to a Soviet attack on Western Europe, and as a means of keeping any potential theater of war outside America. Troop deployment, then, represented not so much a Truman victory as a national safeguard. Indeed, by demonstrating the necessity for restraints on executive authority the debate over the NATO deployment strengthened the political position of McCarthy and his congressional supporters.

᠊ᡃᠥ

ON April 11, 1951, President Truman dramatically dismissed General Douglas MacArthur as commander-in-chief of United Nations forces in Korea. MacArthur's "insubordination" in disobeying executive orders to clear all policy statements with the administration, and his public disagreement with official military strategy in the Korean War, Truman charged, required that the President assert his executive powers to sustain traditional civilian control over the military. More importantly, Truman said, had he not disciplined MacArthur's independent action, which was contrary to official policy, Allied unity would have been undermined and an unnecessarily larger war might have developed. Truman also charged MacArthur with making partisan politics of his policy differences, thereby threatening bipartisanship and possibly frustrating the effective implementation of U.S. foreign policy. McCarthyite support of MacArthur's cause was the evidence of this charge, he said. Truman went on to contend that conservative Republicans were only exploiting the dismissal to advance their influence on the national political scene.

In the MacArthur incident, Truman failed once again to raise popular support for his position. On the one hand, his rebuke of the McCarthyites for partisanship appeared an equally partisan administration effort to silence dissent. On the other, the issue of civilian supremacy seemed only a smokescreen raised to justify a demand for uncontested executive power. Since the Cold War diplomacy developed by Truman himself had made popular the premises of the need for superior military strength, quickness of response, and a policy determined by experts, in the specific circumstances of the Korean conflict it would seem—using Truman's own logic —that it was the military experts, not the civilian politicians, who could best devise policy and most effectively advance the national interest. In the end, the general public viewed MacArthur, not Truman, as the proper expert.

In what proved to be a disastrous political move, the administration justified MacArthur's dismissal on the grounds of ending disunity and divisive debate. On April 28 the Democratic National Committee published a "fact sheet" on the dismissal for the stated purpose of ending "falsification"

through a sane, objective discussion of the issues. Raising national-security themes and emphasizing the administration's
nonpartisan motives, the Committee argued that the Korean
War "involves our national security and the peace of the
world. Many Republican leaders, on the other hand, have
sought from the start to make political capital out of the
necessity, which most of them recognized at the time, for the
free people of the world to resist Communism unless they
were prepared to yield to it." Truman expressed this warning
more forcefully: "This [the Korean War] is not a political
matter. It is a matter of life and death for our country and our
way of life."

The failure of Truman and his fellow Democrats to distinguish between policy and partisanship, the implication that
the administration's Korean War strategy should not be publicly debated, and the attempt to impugn the motives of the
McCarthyites in criticizing MacArthur's dismissal—all this
contributed further to the loss of confidence in the Truman
administration. The nation felt that such serious questions as
how the national security might best be advanced and communism resisted were quite proper subjects of public debate
and deliberation. The complexity of these issues, moreover,
made executive claims to expertise tenuous at best; maximum
deliberation and intelligent discussion were needed in order
to minimize mistakes and ensure the adoption of the most
feasible course. McCarthyites cited earlier administration errors as proof of its fallibility and demanded, in consequence,
increased criticism and surveillance.

A good part of MacArthur's popularity and Truman's un-
popularity derived from public doubts about the wisdom of
a limited-war strategy to begin with. Committed to that
strategy fully, the administration sought to silence any critics
by impugning their motives as essentially partisan. The Mac-
Arthur dismissal allowed McCarthy and his supporters to
criticize the administration for suppressing free speech; it also

enabled them to demand more extended, democratic participation in the formulation or revision of policy.

§❧

THE TIMING OF MacArthur's dismissal coincided with Truman's attempt to restrict public access to executive information. On September 25, 1951, the President issued an Executive Order extending classification procedures from military and intelligence agencies to civilian ones. The purpose of the extension, he stated, was "to strengthen our safeguards against divulging to potential enemies information harmful to the security of the United States." Naturally, Truman denied that the extension constituted a form of censorship or that executive agencies would use it to cover up their mistakes. Asking for public cooperation, and specifically appealing to the patriotism of the press, Truman accused his critics of "misrepresenting" his order; the problem, he asserted, was that too much, and not too little, information had been divulged. As Secretary of Commerce Charles Sawyer later put it: "Our object should be not only the utmost freedom consistent with safety, but the utmost safety consistent with freedom."

To represent classification as the best approach "to a problem that is important to the survival of the United States," and to affirm that every citizen "including officials and publishers—has a duty to protect our country" naturally increased popular anxieties about subversion. Yet these anxieties did not produce any resurgence of support for Truman's new restrictions; instead they raised the question whether his real motive was to avoid surveillance. It seemed to many people that surveillance, not censorship, could best safeguard national security; patriotism required not simply acceptance of administration authority but the uncovering of all wrong-doing.

As in the MacArthur episode, the McCarthyites emerged from the classification issue as the champions of free speech and constitutional rights. Immediately after the President's announcement of the new restrictions, twenty-five conservative Senators released a statement pledging "to rally to the defense of any person against whom reprisals are directed as the result of the exercise of his constitutional right of freedom of speech." The Senators further observed: "There is evidence that some persons or groups in authority in our Government are unable to tolerate criticism. This is manifested by the smear tactics and propaganda techniques now being used to silence any critics." "Uncontrolled public discussion," they continued, "is the American tradition and is the greatest enemy of tyranny. There is evidence that no man can criticize our Government today and escape intemperate reprisals. This is an alarming situation. It cannot be ignored. We, therefore . . . pledge to the American people that we shall fight to guarantee that, in the difficult days ahead, no man's voice shall be silenced."

Much the same confrontation with the McCarthyites occurred when the administration opposed a Senate bill, S. 2255, introduced by McCarthyite Senator Pat McCarran to provide that the records of all officials and employees receiving compensation from the United States Treasury be open to the public and the press, unless specifically exempted through congressional legislation. Conceding that official records were the property of the people, the administration nonetheless argued that secrecy continued to be essential to national security. Only the nation's enemies, the administration warned, would benefit from the publication of national secrets.

This line of argument did not hold up. Although the McCarran bill established maximum information as its priority, it did provide for exceptions to publication that included "national secrets"—subject, of course, to congressional approval. The bill simply required the executive branch to share with Congress information and authority over the publication or restriction of information.

Although never acted upon, the McCarran bill nonetheless clearly revealed the extent of the split between the administration and McCarthyites. This split widened in 1952 when Truman refused to honor two congressional attempts to secure information—by Senator McCarran for the loyalty file of John Carter Vincent and by Representative Frank Chelf for a Department of Justice resumé of the action taken on all civil and criminal cases from 1945 to 1951. Both requests were related to specific committee investigations: McCarran's to a review of the State Department's loyalty program, Chelf's to a study of corruption in the Justice Department. In denying these requests, Truman again cited the need to protect the national interest and preserve the executive prerogatives of the separation of powers and the right to secrecy.

--- ❧ ---

BY 1952 the conflict between the Truman administration and Senator McCarthy and his congressional supporters had transcended simple differences over policy. It had reached the point where neither side would concede the sincerity of the other. The administration-McCarthy conflict attained new heights of bitterness during the 1952 primary and pre-convention campaigns—and particularly over the McCarthyite-supported candidacy of Senator Robert Taft. In his campaign, Taft and his supporters concentrated on the record of the Truman administration, blaming Truman's indecisive foreign policy for contributing to the emergence of the Soviet threat and contending that this had come about through internal subversion. Although the McCarthyites failed in their objective of gaining the Republican nomination for Taft, they did effectively influence the character of the presidential campaign. Because of their general aggressiveness and their influence in shaping the popular image of Republicanism, even Eisenhower's supporters and the Republican National Committee adopted their major themes—albeit in a more restrained, sophisticated manner. In both the primaries and after the convention, Republican presidential campaign strategy centered on the loyalty of Democratic policy-makers and the lack of wisdom of their policies.

Yet in supporting the Democrats' presidential nominee, Adlai Stevenson, Truman in effect spent most of his time defending his own record. Referring almost in passing to Stevenson's abilities and qualifications, he extolled the accomplishments of his administration, the soundness of his policies, the vigor of his anti-communism, and the irresponsibility of his Republican critics. Denying that his policies could have been improved upon, Truman claimed they had in fact greatly advanced the national interest.

As a campaigner for Stevenson, Truman attempted to scare the public about the consequences of a Republican victory. McCarthyite criticisms of his administration's policy, he said, were harmful to national security and represented no more than an effort to divert attention from the Republicans' own "reactionary" record. Almost wholly negative, Truman's campaign strategy centered on attacking the Republican past, recalling the depression, isolationism, and the record of the 80th Congress. His main argument for electing a Democratic President seemed to be that doing so would defeat the Republicans.

Truman's campaign tactics backfired and, indeed, tended to undercut Stevenson's more temperate approach toward winning over the electorate. The Democrats, and Adlai Stevenson in particular, were seriously harmed by the pettiness and petulant tone of Truman's attempts at self-justification. His insistence on the perfection of his administration only afforded McCarthyites more opportunities for detailing its imperfection. Truman's intensely partisan campaigning enabled Eisenhower and the Republicans to assume the stance of disinterested patriots eager to restore a necessary balance to the body politic. It helped put Eisenhower in the White House and a covey of McCarthyites in Congress.

8

The Decline of McCarthyism

THE SPECIFICALLY anti-communist crusade led by the junior Senator from Wisconsin and called McCarthyism in the end turned out to be an ephemeral phenomenon. In large part it was the direct product of the inception of the Cold War and the presidency of Harry S. Truman. When the Eisenhower administration came into office it continued, or at any rate neglected to change, many of those Truman administration policies which McCarthy and his conservative congressional supporters had specifically opposed. Consistency as well as political expediency required that McCarthy and his supporters also denounce the Eisenhower administration. But doing so ultimately undermined their former image of disinterested patriotism; for the nature of their critique reflected less consistency than concern over the loss of a good campaign issue. In stridently attacking their own Republican administration, they inadvertently identified themselves as reactionaries, and thereby disclosed their real character—formerly masked by the announced goal of preserving the national security—as a self-interested, anti–New Deal minority.

This is not to say that the Eisenhower administration ever formally repudiated Senator McCarthy and his conservative adherents, though after 1953 it challenged, if only indirectly, the McCarthyite influence by advancing measures which tacitly repudiated its earlier tolerance of McCarthyism. During the 1952 presidential campaign, Eisenhower and his supporters had found it politically expedient to accept McCarthy's charges of "treason and betrayal" in high places. If for no other reason, not to have done so would have indirectly affirmed the Truman administration's consistent contention between 1950 and 1952 that McCarthy and his conservative congressional supporters were irresponsible, their criticism both inimical to the national interest and wholly partisan in motivation.

Thus, in this limited sense at least, the McCarthyites, though they failed to nominate Taft, did succeed in some rough way in setting the broad guidelines of Eisenhower's campaign. Eisenhower campaigned in 1952 on the need to repudiate the Yalta agreements, to institute a general housecleaning of the State Department, and to end the arbitrary secrecy of the executive branch's conduct of foreign policy and internal security. Eisenhower also expressed mild support for the "liberation" of the Soviet satellite countries and the "unleashing" of Chiang Kai-shek. In one way or another, these campaign promises coincided with prevailing popular fears and concerns originally exploited by McCarthy and his congressional supporters. The character of the campaign was thus in the main a negative one, Eisenhower's election amounting in many respects to a vote of no-confidence in the Truman administration. In addition, of course, Eisenhower's personal appeal and the simplicity of his approach—in contrast to Truman's call for a crusade and Stevenson's sophisticated wit—made him an enormously attractive political personality.

Once the Eisenhower administration took office, however, it no longer enjoyed the luxury of opposition rhetoric. Accordingly, it tempered its earlier campaign criticism lest its failure to act on that criticism result in a loss of its credibility. Specifically, and contrary to Eisenhower's campaign promises, his administration continued the policy of containment, sought and secured a negotiated settlement of the Korean War, and attempted to reach a détente with the Soviet Union. It did not "unleash" Chiang Kai-shek, did not seek to "liberate" Eastern Europe, and did not (despite the attempt to create the impression it had through statements and press releases made by Attorney General Herbert Brownell, Vice-President Richard Nixon, and the Republican National Committee in 1953 and 1954) uncover any communist spy cell or subversives operating in any federal agency, including the State Department. Yet the Eisenhower administration's post-campaign shift to essentially the same policies and priorities of the Truman administration was neither so dramatic nor so blatant as this list implies. In actuality it was a gradual, informal shift which, by carefully obfuscating the grounds for McCarthyite criticism, made that criticism itself appear unwarranted.

But in four specific cases—the appointment of Charles Bohlen as Ambassador to the Soviet Union; the defeat of the Bricker Amendment; the failure to repudiate, or to publish fully, the Yalta agreements; and the convening of the Geneva Conference—the Eisenhower administration and the McCarthyites clashed head-on. In losing each of these confrontations with the Eisenhower administration, the political appeal of the McCarthyites was gradually sapped and, ultimately, destroyed.

§⟶

McCarthyite objections to Bohlen's appointment as Russian Ambassador centered on his service as an interpreter for the United States delegation at the Yalta Conference and his having been regularly identified with the crucial policy decisions of the Truman administration. As if this were not sufficient to incite opposition, Bohlen had also openly defended the Yalta Conference during hearings conducted by

the Senate Foreign Relations Committee on his ambassa-
dorial nomination. Not surprisingly, the combination of the
nomination and Bohlen's testimony posed the issue for the
McCarthyites of whether the new administration was "soft
on communism."

By nominating Bohlen as his ambassador to the Soviet
Union, Eisenhower made it known he wanted a "Yalta man"
for the Russian post, and in the process confirmed—dis-
claimers from Secretary of State John Foster Dulles and
Republican Senator Alexander Wiley notwithstanding—that
his administration would be governed by essentially the same
attitudes and assumptions toward the Soviet Union that the
Truman administration had had. By nominating Bohlen,
Eisenhower was also in effect discounting McCarthyite allegations about the disloyalty of Democratic policy-makers and
the lax security procedures of the Truman administration. At
all events, Bohlen's nomination was certainly not consistent
with Eisenhower's campaign promise totally to purge the
State Department and the Foreign Service.

When the Bohlen nomination reached the floor of Congress, it temporarily split the McCarthyites. The more moderate among them supported it; the more extreme did not.
As Ambassador to Moscow, such moderately McCarthyite
senators as Taft, Capehart, and Watkins maintained, Bohlen's
role would be roughly identical to the one he had played at
Yalta: that of functionary rather than policy-maker. They also
made Bohlen's confirmation an issue of the President's
authority and integrity. Eisenhower, they claimed, had both
the right to select ambassadors and the duty to preserve the
independence and morale of an essentially loyal Foreign
Service.

The main substance of the extremist McCarthyite opposition (led by McCarthy himself, Bridges, Dirksen, Jenner, and
Welker) was that Bohlen was a security risk. Yet they were
unable to substantiate their charges that Bohlen was disloyal

or had subversive proclivities, nor could they discredit his eminent qualifications for the ambassadorship. In contrast to the administration's well-developed case for Bohlen's nomination, their evidence was thin, resting solely on Bohlen's role at Yalta and the inclusion of certain unsubstantiated derogatory information in his loyalty file.

This latter evidence was easily defused in early 1953. A specially appointed subcommittee of the Senate Foreign Relations Committee, composed of Robert Taft and John Sparkman, had requested administration authorization to examine Bohlen's loyalty file. Secretary of State Dulles granted this request, at the same time making it known that this was to be an exception to departmental policy. After reviewing Bohlen's file, Taft assured the Senate that his loyalty could not be doubted. The derogatory information contained in his file, Taft said, was either unsubstantiated or involved purely political, as opposed to security, considerations.

Taft's defense of Bohlen put his nomination beyond dispute. Taft's conservative credentials, his stand in the 1952 campaign, his unquestioned personal integrity, and his vigorous anti-communism not only stifled the effort to deny Bohlen the nomination but, more importantly, disclosed the essential irrelevancy of McCarthy's old tactic of quoting derogatory comments from the loyalty reports. (The subsequent Army-McCarthy hearings established this even more dramatically.) In the future the McCarthyites would need stronger evidence; when they failed to produce it, the failure was costly.

ॐ

THE BOHLEN NOMINATION formally revealed the divergent interests and objectives of McCarthyites and the Eisenhower administration. Subsequent developments in 1954 and 1955 widened this rift, dramatizing the anti-reformist tactics and intransigent nature of the McCarthyites. This revelation tended further to isolate them politically.

In 1954 the Eisenhower administration opposed a proposed constitutional amendment that had been introduced off and on since 1951 by the McCarthyite Senator John Bricker (Republican, Ohio). The stated purpose of the Bricker Amendment was to restrict executive authority on foreign policy by requiring congressional ratification (both House and Senate) of any foreign treaty or executive agreement that had relevance to domestic politics. With Roosevelt's and Truman's autocratic independence still fresh in mind, the Republican party in 1952 had gone on record supporting such restrictions.

In proposing his amendment, however, Bricker's objective was not simply to check executive authority; he also hoped to curb the reformist influence of international commitments on domestic events. Specifically, Bricker and other McCarthyites were concerned that United States ratification of the World Health Organization and the U.N. Covenant on Human Rights would result in both federally supported medical care and federal intervention to end Southern segregation.

In contrast to Republican support for the Bricker Amendment in 1951 (moderates and conservatives alike lined up for Bricker, including John Foster Dulles), the Eisenhower administration opposed it in 1954 on the grounds that it would cripple the operation of foreign policy and, by reducing executive flexibility, impair the national security (essentially, it should be noted, a Truman argument). The effect of administration opposition to the Bricker Amendment was to bring back the national-security debate. In this recast debate the McCarthyites' role of defenders of Americanism and national security seemed considerably blurred; they now appeared to be only self-interested conservatives seeking arbitrarily to restrict the powers of the President.

Bricker's amendment was never voted upon by the Senate.

Instead, on February 26, 1954, an amendment to the amendment, proposed by Senator Walter George (Democrat, Georgia), failed to secure the necessary two-thirds majority in the Senate.*

ॐ

DURING THE 1952 campaign and in his State of the Union address in 1953, Eisenhower alluded to the need to repudiate secret international agreements. Attractive as campaign rhetoric, this suggestion did not, however, become administration policy. For one thing, repudiation of former agreements —specifically of the Yalta agreement—would not result in the "liberation" of either Eastern Europe or China. For another, such repudiation would be considered a provocative action by the Soviet Union, and would thus only increase Cold War tensions. It would also harm United States relations with the NATO countries. Moreover, the unilateral abrogation of earlier commitments ran counter to the administration's stated objective of adhering to established international procedures. For all these reasons, in February 1953 the Eisenhower administration recommended to Congress a resolution criticizing the Soviet Union for violating the terms of the Yalta agreements. But it did not repudiate the agreements themselves.

In substance this resolution—House Joint Resolution 200, introduced by John Vorys (Republican, Ohio), chairman of the House Committee on Foreign Affairs—repeated arguments used consistently since 1950 by the Democrats to

---

*George's amendment would have required congressional approval of all treaties and executive agreements affecting domestic law. This amendment sought to shift the focus of the debate from executive foreign policy authority *per se,* as in Bricker's original proposal, to the effect of international agreements on domestic law.

defend Yalta against McCarthyite criticism. Moreover, the resolution was supported by the Democrats. Confronted by the potentially embarrassing prospect of affirming an earlier Democratic apologia for Yalta, and yet unwilling to reject or amend the Eisenhower-proposed resolution for fear of seeming narrowly partisan, McCarthyites killed the resolution in committee. They thus avoided a divisive debate that might compromise their relations with Eisenhower or force him to press for its enactment. In the end, Eisenhower's failure to repudiate Yalta—or even to come out criticizing the Soviets for violating its terms—when the Republicans commanded a majority in both houses redounded to the McCarthyites' disadvantage. Thereafter, any McCarthyite assault on Democratic "betrayal" was less effective: in retaliation, the Democrats could raise both the nature of the failed resolution and subsequent congressional inaction on Yalta as proof of (unjustifiable) McCarthyite partisanship against the Truman administration.

Moreover, once the Eisenhower administration released the full text of the Yalta proceedings in 1955, it seriously undercut much of the basis of the McCarthyites' prestige. The post-1949 controversy over Roosevelt's "secret" diplomacy at Yalta had enabled McCarthyites to charge that further Yalta agreements existed, and that these agreements had in large measure been responsible for Soviet expansion. In fact, it was this charge that first enlisted major public support for the McCarthyites. Thus, in publishing the Yalta proceedings and revealing that no further secret agreements existed, Eisenhower greatly undermined the McCarthyites' credibility.

Although McCarthy and other conservative Congressmen immediately accused the Eisenhower administration of censoring the Yalta papers, specifically laying the blame on State Department holdovers from the Acheson years, Eisenhower's public image of respectability and integrity served to confound the charge. In effect, publication of the papers demolished Yalta as a major national political issue. It also demonstrated the McCarthyites' essentially anti-reformist purposes. No one could seriously believe that a Republican administration would censor the Yalta papers to protect Roosevelt's reputation. It was becomingly increasingly apparent that the McCarthyites were—and had been since 1945—beating dead horses, if not altogether imaginary ones.

THE EISENHOWER administration essentially guaranteed the political isolation of Senator McCarthy and his followers when it decided to meet with the Soviet leaders at Geneva in 1955. A significant shift away from the Holy War atmosphere of the late 1940's and early 1950's, the Geneva Conference represented both an administration rejection of the "victory-over-communism" school and a willingness to trust the Soviets. It also represented a tacit acceptance of the reality of Russia's power and its importance as an international force. Hoping to reach some form of agreement with the Soviets consistent with its definition of American interests, the Eisenhower administration had set out to prove that negotiation—that McCarthyite *bête noire*—was neither inherently beneficial to the Soviets nor inherently harmful to American interests.

Naturally enough, McCarthy and other congressional conservatives very bitterly condemned the Geneva Conference. Insofar as it was an effort to reduce Cold War tensions and differences through diplomacy, the conference subverted the validity of the old McCarthyite (and Truman) policy of confrontation and intransigence. Although the Geneva Conference only slightly mitigated Cold War tensions, McCarthy's and his supporters' continued criticism, their simple reiteration of sour anti-communist slogans, and their denunciation of any effort to reach agreement with the Soviets only dramatized the anachronistic narrowness and conservatism of their movement. The national security they had so vigorously defended against communism and Democratic "appeasement" had in no way been harmed by negotiation *with* communists in 1955. In fact, negotiation had served the national interest, offering the prospect of averting a suicidal third world war by substituting rationality for inflexibility. By 1955 the public was coming to realize that one did not have to call for the annihilation of communism to be an anticommunist. The Eisenhower administration had through such actions as these begun to alter the public mood.

IN THE final analysis, McCarthyite criticisms of the Eisenhower administration, which were essentially a repetition of the tactics and charges directed at the more vulnerable Truman administration, were counterproductive. By attacking Eisenhower, McCarthy and other conservative Congressmen overstepped the bounds of their popular support. The public did not mistrust Eisenhower as it had Truman, and certainly not in the early years of his administration when McCarthy unwisely launched his attack. Eisenhower's tremendous popularity, the absence of any dramatic evidence of personnel disloyalty in his administration, and the public's gradual if reluctant acceptance of the possibility of negotiating with the Soviet Union had by 1955 rendered McCarthy's and the McCarthyites' tactics ineffective—if not offensive. In fact, McCarthyite attacks on the Eisenhower administration only enhanced the administration's standing with the public. In contrast to McCarthy's frenzied tone and shotgun charges— particularly in the Army hearings of 1954, his Waterloo—the administration appeared a veritable repository of reason and moderation.

Eisenhower was not Truman, and it was Truman and such

Cold War liberals as Acheson and McGrath who, by heightening popular fears of communism and raising distrust about executive priorities and methods, had helped to create the phenomenon of McCarthyism. Eisenhower's election and his subsequent foreign policy decisions reduced the effectiveness of McCarthyite charges and dramatically, though unintentionally, revealed McCarthyism to be an irresponsible force in American politics. McCarthy's former image of objectivity was thereby destroyed. Yet to the extent that absolute security and containment remained basic objectives of United States policy, post-1955 foreign policy debate remained narrowly circumscribed. In that sense, the tactics of Joseph McCarthy and his supporters of pointing out guilt by association and charging leaders with being "soft on communism" continued to be an essential part of national politics. The immediate and direct impact of McCarthyism might have been reduced, but even today it lingers on as a conservative force in American political life.

Appendices

ALTHOUGH public opinion polls can provide insights into changing popular attitudes, they are of decidedly limited value. The questions asked by the pollsters, and their phrasing of these questions, affect the response without necessarily establishing a conscious popular concern. Thus, in the polls cited in these appendices, many of the questions were phrased in rhetoric similar to that used by President Truman to justify particular policy decisions—as in the economic focus of the Truman Doctrine—or to that used by key congressional committees—as in the depiction of the 1948 HUAC investigation as the "communist spy hearings." Conceding these drawbacks, the polls nonetheless reinforce my thesis in disclosing a qualitative change in the nature of popular anti-communism. They confirm an anti-Soviet stance that was less militant in 1945 than in 1951, and a public that, while it responded to McCarthy's explanation of postwar problems as a conspiracy of "communists in government," also continued to support summit diplomacy and efforts to negotiate differences.

The polls cited in these appendices were all published in the *Public Opinion Quarterly* during the years 1945 to 1951, and were derived from major polling organizations. I have in every case paraphrased the questions and the public response. The total response sometimes does not equal 100 per cent as I have not always reported "no opinion" or miscellaneous responses where these responses were not significant. I have included specific quotes when the phrasing of the question was slanted or the response striking. As a means of illustrating the nature of popular Cold War attitudes on what became the major issues exploited by the McCarthyites, I have divided these questions into two areas—foreign policy and internal security. I have further subdivided these topics into popular attitudes toward: (1) the desirability of détente or negotiations with the Soviet Union; (2) Truman's containment policies; (3) U.S. policy toward the Soviet Union; (4) the administration's Far Eastern policy; (5) domestic communism; and (6) the administration's loyalty-security policies.

APPENDIX I

Popular Attitudes Concerning Foreign Policy

A. The Desirability of Détente or Negotiations with the Soviet Union

1945

In March, 55 per cent affirmed that the Soviet Union could be trusted to cooperate with the United States after the war; 31 per cent did not.

By June, 45 per cent affirmed that the Soviet Union could be trusted to cooperate with the United States after the war; 38 per cent did not.

26 per cent maintained that the United States should have the most say in the United Nations, but only 12 per cent thought that this would in fact result.

Similarly, 19 per cent maintained that the United States, the Soviet Union, and Great Britain should have the most say in the United Nations, and 49 per cent thought that this would result.

81 per cent supported the United States joining the United Nations, while 11 per cent did not.

43 per cent believed that the United States should rely on the atomic bomb for defense, 48 per cent on world organization.

31 per cent favored a large United States standing army to preserve the peace, 56 per cent a world peace force.

38.6 per cent described the Soviet Union as a peace-loving nation with defensive aims, 37.8 per cent an aggressive nation, and 8.4 per cent both a defensive and aggressive nation.

22.7 per cent deemed it necessary that every possible effort be made to insure friendly relations with the Soviet Union, 49.2 per cent opposed "too many" concessions to attaining necessary friendly relations, and 11.3 per cent that the United States should welcome but make no special effort to insure friendly relations.

42.4 per cent believed that U.S.-Soviet relations would improve in the future, 23.5 per cent that they would remain the same, and 19.1 per cent that they would worsen.

1946

49 per cent believed that the Big Three could work together in a world government; 39 per cent did not.

55 per cent maintained that the United Nations would be able to preserve the peace for the next twenty-five years; 25 per cent did not.

54 per cent supported and 24 per cent opposed strengthening the United Nations to make it a world government with a world police force.

50 per cent expressed unfavorable and 17 per cent sympathetic views about Soviet policies toward other countries.

58 per cent maintained that the purpose of Soviet military strength was to achieve world power, 29 per cent for protection.

Yet 42 per cent maintained that Soviet actions revealed a concern over security, 26 per cent over "imperialist" expansion.

Later in the year, 33.8 per cent described Soviet military build-up as defensive intended to avert an attack, 50 per cent as intended to attain world domination.

73 per cent doubted that U.S.-Soviet differences were so major that war was inevitable, 17 per cent believed that they were.

18 per cent approved and 40 per cent disapproved of Winston Churchill's "iron curtain" speech in Fulton, Missouri.

Yet 83 per cent supported and 10 per cent opposed a U.S.-British military alliance.

At the same time, 52 per cent supported and 34 per cent opposed a U.S.-Soviet military alliance.

15.4 per cent deemed it necessary that the United States secure good terms with the Soviet Union, 52.3 per cent did not believe that the United States should make major concessions to attain desirable terms, and 15.1 per cent maintained that the United States should not make a special effort to attain good terms.

24 per cent described the United States, Great Britain, and Soviet Union as allies, while 50 per cent maintained that their wartime friendship had disappeared.

1947

6 per cent believed that United States policy should attempt to

strengthen the United Nations, 28 per cent that it should rely on atomic capabilities.

10 per cent believed that the United States should give up on the United Nations and instead rely on bilateral alliances, 55 per cent favored reliance on the United Nations, and 17 per cent supported world government.

62 per cent favored continued cooperation with the Soviet Union to attain an effective international organization; 31 per cent deemed Soviet exclusion essential to the effectiveness of the United Nations.

74 per cent maintained that both the United States and the Soviet Union were responsible for prevailing tensions; 17 per cent believed that only one nation was responsible.

1948

63 per cent favored the convening of an international conference with the Soviet Union to work out the basis for peace, 28 per cent deemed this a poor idea, while 9 per cent had no opinion.

At the same time, only 34 per cent believed that such a meeting would succeed, 5 per cent that it would be a qualified success, 35 per cent that it would be a failure, and 26 per cent had no opinion.

1949

50 per cent believed that there would be a war within the next twenty-five years, 41 per cent that a war could be avoided.

In August (before the announcement of the Soviet atomic bomb explosion), 20 per cent maintained that the United States should declare its intent not to use the atomic bomb unless first used by another state, 70 per cent opposed issuing such a statement, and 5 per cent advocated outlawing the bomb.

1950

In March, 68 per cent believed that before attempting to develop a hydrogen bomb efforts should be made to attain agreement on atomic control, 23 per cent opposed such a prior attempt, and 9 per cent had no opinion.

In October, after the outbreak of the Korean War, 52 per cent deemed a Truman-Stalin meeting a good idea, 35 per cent a poor idea, 6 per cent a fair idea, while 7 per cent had no opinion.

Yet only 21 per cent believed such a meeting would succeed, 61 per cent did not, and 18 per cent didn't know.

1951

76 per cent believed that a Truman-Stalin meeting was a good idea, 10 per cent a bad idea, and 14 per cent had no opinion.

B. Truman's Containment Policies

1947

56 per cent approved and 32 per cent disapproved of the Truman Doctrine, while 12 per cent had no opinion.

Yet 83 per cent approved and 14 per cent disapproved sending U.S. civilian experts to Greece to supervise the use of economic aid.

And only 33 per cent approved and 54 per cent disapproved sending U.S. military advisers to train the Greek royalist army.

Moreover, 37 per cent supported and 53 per cent opposed providing military aid to Greece.

38 per cent believed it likely and 55 per cent unlikely that aid to Greece and Turkey would lead to war.

24 per cent believed the general purpose of the Truman Doctrine was to stop communism, 7 per cent to support democracy, and 35 per cent to promote relief, rehabilitation, and humanitarian purposes.

In September, queried what U.S. policy should be if military aid to Greece and Turkey were not enough, 4 per cent believed that the United States should "allow" the Soviet Union to control Greece, 6 per cent allow the Soviet Union to control Greece but plan to stop any future Soviet effort to control other countries, 28 per cent bring the matter to the United Nations for armed border patrols, and 40 per cent use the United Nations as a forum for warning the Soviet Union that any further incursions into Greece would lead to a declaration of war.

1948

56 per cent believed that the Marshall Plan was designed to assist Europe, 8 per cent to curb communism, 20 per cent to further trade with Europe, while 26 per cent had no opinion.

68 per cent favored and 19 per cent opposed the formation of a Western European military alliance, while 13 per cent had no opinion.

1949

24 per cent responded that NATO would increase the likelihood of war with the Soviet Union, 43 per cent would decrease, 11 per cent would make no difference, and 22 per cent had no opinion.

53 per cent described NATO as a defensive alliance, 5 per cent an alliance for an attack on the Soviet Union, 7 per cent expressed no opinion, and 35 per cent expressed unfamiliarity with the NATO Pact.

56 per cent supported and 31 per cent opposed a blanket U.S. pledge to aid another nation if it were attacked.

53 per cent supported and 32 per cent opposed U.S. military aid to a nation if it were threatened by an internal attack

And 40 per cent supported and 48 per cent opposed promising aid to another nation were it attacked.

33 per cent supported and 18 per cent opposed sending military aid to Western Europe, 7 per cent had no opinion, and 42 per cent were unfamiliar with NATO.

46 per cent supported and 40 per cent opposed supplying arms and money to those nations willing to build up their armies as protection against the Soviet Union, while 14 per cent had no opinion.

1950

57 per cent believed that with the Korean War the United States was involved in a Third World War, 28 per cent that the conflict could be localized, while 15 per cent had no opinion.

20 per cent described U.S. involvement in the Korean War as a mistake, 65 per cent disagreed, and 15 per cent had no opinion.

27 per cent believed that United Nations' troops should stop at the 38th parallel, 64 per cent should continue beyond the parallel, and 9 per cent had no opinion.

46 per cent believed that even if China entered the Korean War that the conflict could be localized, 39 per cent favored going into China.

Yet 57 per cent supported and only 28 per cent opposed abiding by a United Nations vote permitting China to be seated in the U.N. in return for her withdrawal from the Korean War, while 15 per cent had no opinion.

81 per cent maintained that China had intervened on orders from Moscow, 5 per cent disagreed, and 14 per cent had no opinion.

80 per cent maintained that United States security would be affected if Western Europe went Communist, 10 per cent did not, while 10 per cent had no opinion.

62 per cent believed that West Germany would go Communist if U.S. troops were withdrawn, 17 per cent did not, and 21 per cent didn't know.

1951

68 per cent supported a U.S. troop withdrawal and only 23 per cent remaining in Korea.

55 per cent believed the sending of U.S. troops to South Korea to stop Communist aggression was right, 36 per cent wrong, and 9 per cent had no opinion.

Yet 50 per cent described U.S. involvement in the Korean War as a mistake, 39 per cent did not, and 11 per cent had no opinion.

In April, 56 per cent believed that the United States should try harder to reach an agreement with China and North Korea and only 34 per cent disagreed.

73 per cent maintained that the United States should accept a cease-fire if the Chinese and North Koreans accepted the 38th parallel, and only 16 per cent were opposed.

64 per cent approved requiring congressional assent prior to assigning U.S. troops to Europe, 28 per cent believed that the President should retain this authority, and 8 per cent were undecided.

C. United States Policy Toward the Soviet Union

1946

61 per cent favored a policy of firmness, 11 per cent of understanding, toward the Soviet Union.

1947

42 per cent maintained that newspaper accounts made the Soviet Union appear worse than it really was, 17 per cent better, 21 per cent a fair picture, and 20 per cent didn't know.

41 per cent believed that the United States dealt with the Soviet Union in an intelligent manner, 32 per cent did not, and 27 per cent had no opinion.

62 per cent believed U.S. policy toward the Soviet Union was too soft, 6 per cent too hard, 24 per cent about right, while 8 per cent had no opinion.

1948

73 per cent believed U.S. policy toward the Soviet Union was too soft, 3 per cent too hard, 11 per cent about right, and 13 per cent had no opinion.

At the same time, only 17 per cent believed that Truman was "giving in" to the Russians, 53 per cent was opposed to giving in, 4 per cent had no opinion, and 26 per cent didn't know.

18 per cent maintained that the United States should be more willing to cooperate with the Soviet Union, 26 per cent that official policy was about right, 53 per cent demanded a firmer policy, and 11 per cent were undecided.

Yet when queried how a firmer policy could best be achieved: only 6 per cent recommended strengthening the armed forces, 13 per cent a stronger diplomatic position, and 12 per cent a stronger economic policy.

47 per cent approved and 37 per cent disapproved United States' efforts to suppress Communist-led revolts to seize control of governments by force, while 16 per cent had no opinion.

54 per cent maintained that the United States should and 39 per cent should not attempt to stop any Soviet effort to control bordering territories in Europe or Asia, while 7 per cent were undecided.

28.3 per cent maintained that the United States should and 52.2 per cent should not intervene militarily should the Italian Communists win control through elections in Italy.

1950

50 per cent doubted that the Soviet Union wanted war with the

United States, 35 per cent believed that she did, and 17 per cent had no opinion.

In May, only 16 per cent believed that the United States was winning the Cold War, 23 per cent the Soviet Union, 5 per cent neither, 14 per cent didn't know, while 42 per cent were unfamiliar with the term Cold War.

1951

30 per cent believed that the Soviet Union was winning the Cold War, only 9 per cent the United States, 12 per cent neither, 4 per cent had no opinion, while 45 per cent were unfamiliar with the term Cold War.

D. Administration Far Eastern Policy

1945

65 per cent supported Soviet involvement in the Far Eastern war following the conclusion of the European war, and only 22 per cent believed that the Soviet Union should remain neutral.

1948

In April, 55 per cent approved and 32 per cent disapproved of U.S. military aid to China, while 13 per cent had no opinion.

By December, 51 per cent maintained that the Chinese Communists took orders from Moscow, 10 per cent did not, while 18 per cent had no opinion.

Moreover, 45 per cent believed that developments in China threatened world peace, 22 per cent did not, and 12 per cent had no opinion.

Yet only 28 per cent supported and 34 per cent opposed U.S. aid to Chiang Kai-shek, 4 per cent expressed qualified approval, and 13 per cent had no opinion.

1949

In May, 43 per cent opposed U.S. involvement in the Chinese civil war, 4 per cent believed China a lost cause, 22 per cent supported providing economic or military aid, and 14 per cent didn't know.

In September, only 8 per cent favored general U.S. aid to keep China from going Communist, 7 per cent military aid, 4 per cent economic aid, 2 per cent propaganda aid, 36 per cent opposed any aid, and 45 per cent didn't know.

And 25 per cent believed that the United States should support Chiang Kai-shek, 44 per cent were opposed, and 31 per cent had no opinion.

1950

In August, 48 per cent supported and 35 per cent opposed U.S. military aid to Chiang Kai-shek, 17 per cent had no opinion.

1951

54 per cent supported and 32 per cent opposed U.S. military aid to Chiang Kai-shek, 14 per cent had no opinion.

APPENDIX II

Popular Attitudes Concerning Internal Security

A. Domestic Communism

1946

49 per cent believed that Communists should be allowed to speak on the radio in peacetime, 39 per cent disagreed, and 12 per cent were undecided.

17 per cent supported and 69 per cent opposed allowing Communists to hold civil service jobs, while 14 per cent had no opinion.

23 per cent believed that American Communists were loyal to the United States, 48 per cent to the Soviet Union, and 29 per cent had no opinion.

1947

In April, 18 per cent believed American Communists were loyal to the United States, 61 per cent to the Soviet Union, while 21 per cent had no opinion.

By December, 19 per cent believed American Communists were loyal to the United States, 59 per cent to the Soviet Union, while 22 per cent had no opinion.

1948

40 per cent did not believe that American Communists threatened the national security, while 45 per cent believed that the Communist Party posed a strong or a potential threat.

In January, 16 per cent believed American Communists were loyal to the United States, 65 per cent to the Soviet Union, and 19 per cent had no opinion.

By June, 23 per cent believed that American Communists were loyal to the United States, 56 per cent to the Soviet Union, and 21 per cent had no opinion.

36 per cent favored and 57 per cent opposed allowing Communists to speak on the radio, while 7 per cent were undecided.

B. *Administration Loyalty-Security Policies*

1946

78 per cent believed that the Soviet Union had spies at work in the United States, 5 per cent did not, and 17 per cent had no opinion.

36 per cent supported the adoption of strong anti-Communist measures (jail, shooting, deportation, registration), 16 per cent only legislation prohibiting Communists from holding public office, 7 per cent while agreeing that Communists should be allowed to hold public office advocated strict surveillance, 16 per cent believed that nothing need be done, and 25 per cent had no opinion.

1947

67 per cent opposed allowing Communists to hold public office, 19 per cent believed that Communists should have the same rights as other citizens, while 14 per cent had no opinion.

69 per cent believed that Truman was and 8 per cent that he was not in favor of excluding Communists from government.

62 per cent supported and 23 per cent opposed legislation forbidding Communist Party membership, and 15 per cent had no opinion.

68 per cent maintained that an employee accused of disloyalty should be permitted to present his case, 24 per cent that an accused employee should be summarily dismissed, and 8 per cent had no opinion.

41 per cent opposed and 36 per cent supported legislation preventing Communist sympathizers from holding public office, 23 per cent had no opinion.

1948

In January, 77 per cent supported and 17 per cent opposed legislation requiring the registration of Communist Party membership.

By June, only 63 per cent supported and 22 per cent opposed a registration measure, while 15 per cent had no opinion.

67 per cent supported and 19 per cent opposed legislation forbidding Communists from holding civil service positions.

74 per cent affirmed that the "Communist spy hearings" (those

conducted by the House Committee on Un-American Activities) were "proving something" and 17 per cent that they were "purely politics."

1949

83 per cent supported and 9 per cent opposed legislation requiring the registration of Communist Party membership, while 8 per cent had no opinion.

80 per cent supported and 10 per cent opposed legislation requiring union officials to sign a non-Communist affidavit; 10 per cent had no opinion.

73 per cent believed that teachers should not and 15 per cent should be allowed to be Communists; 12 per cent had no opinion.

68 per cent supported and 21 per cent opposed legislation forbidding Communist Party membership; 11 per cent had no opinion.

1950

In May, 29 per cent affirmed that McCarthy's charges were harmful and 39 per cent beneficial to the national security, while 16 per cent had no opinion, while 16 per cent were unfamiliar with the Senator's charges.

By July, 22 per cent hadn't heard of McCarthy's charges, 31 per cent approved or believed them, 10 per cent expressed qualified approval, 20 per cent disapproved or disbelieved them, 6 per cent believed that McCarthy was sometimes right and sometimes wrong, and 11 per cent had no opinion.

In August, in the event of a U.S.-Soviet war, 22 per cent believed that American Communists should be interned, 18 per cent imprisoned, 15 per cent sent into exile, 13 per cent sent to the Soviet Union, 13 per cent shot or hung, 4 per cent required to register their membership, 1 per cent advocated doing nothing on grounds of freedom of thought, and 10 per cent had no opinion.

A Note on Sources

DESPITE THE ABSENCE of source citations in the text, this study has been based almost exclusively upon primary source materials. These include the papers and files of Truman administration personnel deposited at the Truman Library, the campaign pamphlets of the Democratic and Republican National Committees and their related congressional and senatorial committees, campaign speeches, congressional debates and hearings, and the news stories, columns, and editorials of selected newspapers and periodicals.

By omitting source notes I hoped to direct the book essentially to a nonacademic audience. For the reader interested in the sources that have been used, I have provided documentation in my other published writings. These include *The Yalta Myths: An Issue in U.S. Politics, 1945–1955* (Columbia, Mo.: University of Missouri Press, 1970), an analysis of the postwar foreign-policy debate and the position of conservative Republicans, identified in this study as McCarthyites, on major foreign policy and loyalty issues; "The Rhetoric of Politics; Foreign Policy, Internal Security, and Domestic Politics in the Truman Era, 1945–1950," and "The Escalation of the Loyalty Program," two essays in *Politics and Policies of the Truman Administration*, edited by Barton J. Bernstein (Chicago: Quadrangle Books, 1970); "The Threat to Civil Liberties: A Study of Selected Criticisms of the Truman Administration's Loyalty Procedures," in *Cold War Critics*, edited by Thomas G. Paterson (Chicago: Quadrangle Books, 1971), an examination of the role of Truman's rhetoric, priorities, and foreign and internal-security policy decisions in contributing to the climate of McCarthyism; "James F. Byrnes: Unwitting Yalta Myth-Maker," *Political Science Quarterly* (December 1966), pp. 581–592, an analysis of Byrnes's alleged "ignorance" about the Yalta Far Eastern agreements; and "Document: Attorney General Clark, Internal Security and the Truman Administration," *New University Thought* (Spring 1968), pp. 16–23, and "The 'National Security' Justification for Electronic Eavesdropping: An Elusive Exception," *Wayne Law*

Review (Summer 1968), pp. 749–772, an investigation of the roles of Attorney General Clark and the Department of Justice in the area of internal security, particularly as this involved the resort to wiretapping.

There are real limits to my research, however, that require clarification. The student of the Cold War, unlike other scholars, cannot gain access to many primary sources (whether government documents or the private papers of key individuals) because of national security prohibitions or classification. While these restrictions have been relaxed over the years, they do remain and necessarily limit our knowledge of historic decisions. This guardedness has in turn set a precedent for the handling of the private papers of important political personalities. Thus, while national-security restrictions apply only to papers controlled by the federal government (e.g., those of the Departments of State, Defense, and Justice), similar standards of use have been imposed on private papers and files (e.g., those presently deposited at the Truman Library). Moreover, the papers and files used by President Truman to write his *Memoirs* still remain in his personal possession and are not yet open to research. In just the same way, the papers of Senator McCarthy, deposited at the Marquette University Library by Mrs. McCarthy, have not been opened for research and study.

Historians of the Cold War are nevertheless not wholly shut out of the primary sources of this critical period in American history. Although important papers of the State, Defense, and Justice Departments are presently closed to scholarship, the State Department has published the *Foreign Relations* series covering wartime and immediate postwar diplomacy through 1945, and other papers have been opened for research. The lifting of all security restrictions is not likely despite the recent (1966) congressional enactment of the Freedom of Information Act. A security-conscious atmosphere persists, and federal personnel are reluctant to lose the immunity provided by the "national security" classification. But the sheer volume of valuable information now available makes these restrictions and their continuance less prohibitive.

Not only can the groundwork for future exploration be laid, but basic research in available papers can be richly rewarding. In part, they are open because of the decision of many important officials to turn their papers over to university libraries. The more valuable collections include those of James Forrestal and Bernard Baruch at Princeton University; Henry Stimson at Yale University; Joseph Grew at Harvard University; William Leahy and Joseph Davies at the Library of Congress; and Arthur Vandenberg at University of Michigan.

Perhaps the most valuable collection is the Truman Library in Independence, Missouri. Its holdings are extensive, including the files and papers not only of the President and important members of his Cabinet and the Democratic National Committee but of the White House staff as well. The library's resources are least valuable in the area of foreign policy. This deficiency stems partially from Truman's continued control over certain presidential papers and from national security restrictions; and partially from the absence of the papers of Truman's Secretaries of State. James F. Byrnes retains possession of his own papers which are to be turned over to the University of South Carolina Library. Edward R. Stettinius' papers are deposited at the University of Virginia Library, George C. Marshall's at the Marshall Library. Although Dean G. Acheson has expressed his intention to turn over his papers to the Truman Library after completion of his memoirs, he has not yet done so.

The resources of the Truman Library in the area of internal security are quite valuable, primarily because of the excellent files of presidential assistants and the two presidential commissions established in 1946 and 1951. Far less valuable are the library's holdings of the papers of Truman's Attorneys General Tom C. Clark and J. Howard McGrath. Clark and McGrath deposited their papers at the library, but these collections consist primarily of the Attorneys General's speech files and selected correspondence (McGrath's papers include his tenure as Democratic National Committee chairman). Significantly absent from McGrath's and Clark's papers are interdepartmental memoranda and other files that would shed light on departmental policy decisions and priorities.

Judged, then, in light of the dominant personalities of the Truman administration, the holdings of the Truman Library are of limited value. Its most important—and accessible—papers are those of subordinate officials and particularly the White House staff. In many cases these papers contain the working drafts and memoranda that provided the basis for administration policy. They are perhaps even more revealing than the papers of the

President, being the day-to-day records of subordinates who dealt with ongoing concerns and decisions. Instructed by the President to explore a specific matter, or delegated responsibility to co-ordinate relations within the executive branch on policy matters or between the executive branch and Congress, the White House staff has provided the historian with a written record of many oral presidential decisions. The papers are, moreover, indirectly revealing about the priorities and concerns which underlay the President's various decisions. The most valuable collections are those of Truman's Legal Counsels, Clark Clifford and Charles Murphy, and White House assistants David Lloyd, Stephen Spingarn, George Elsey, Richard Neustadt, and Philleo Nash. Other sources that I found important were the papers of Theo-dore Tannenwald, assistant to Mutual Security Director W. Averell Harriman; Joseph Jones, a member of the State Depart-ment planning staff in the crucial year 1947; Assistant Secretary of State William Clayton; the Bureau of the Budget legislative files; the Democratic National Committee; the President's Com-mission on Internal Security and Individual Rights; and the Temporary Commission on Employee Loyalty. The files of the Democratic National Committee proved to be valuable for both Democratic and Republican campaign strategy. Because they included extensive holdings of Republican campaign pamphlets, these files supplemented my own research in the files of the Republican National Committee, Republican Senate Policy Com-mittee, and the Republican Congressional Committee. In addi-tion, I examined the Library of Congress' holdings of Democratic and Republican campaign documents, which are surprisingly incomplete and unrepresentative of the major campaign themes.

Another extremely useful source for this study, particularly because of its focus on presidential rhetoric, was the *Public Papers of the Presidents: Harry S. Truman*, vols. 1945–1953 (Washington: U.S. Government Printing Office, 1961–1966). The *Papers* contain the transcripts of Truman's press confer-ences, public addresses, statements, and published correspond-ence. The polls conducted and published by the *Public Opinion Quarterly* provided insights into the temper of the postwar foreign and internal-security debates and into changing popular attitudes. I have further relied upon the *Congressional Record* and on the published hearings and reports of the Senate Foreign Relations Committee, the House Foreign Affairs Committee, the

House Committee on Un-American Activities, the Senate Internal Security Subcommittee, the Senate and House Judiciary Committees, and the Senate and House Armed Services Committees. I have extensively researched press reactions to the events of this period in the *New York Times, Chicago Tribune, Chicago Herald-American, Milwaukee Sentinel, Time, Newsweek, U.S. News and World Report, Saturday Evening Post, New Republic,* and *The Nation.*

Finally, I have relied upon the many studies published either contemporaneously or more recently. These books clarified the major concerns of conservatives and liberals during this period, and increased my understanding of key events and decisions. Conceding the inevitability of some overlap, I have broadly classified these published works into four categories: Foreign Policy, Loyalty-Security, McCarthyism, and the Truman Administration.

Foreign Policy

The consensus on the wisdom and necessity of the Truman administration's containment policy, which formerly characterized the historiography of the Cold War, has recently come under critical scrutiny by younger historians. As the passions of the Cold War have cooled and as historians have acquired access to primary sources, administration policy statements have been reappraised. A more skeptical and critical "revisionist" interpretation now challenges the containment policy. Provocative and controversial, this interpretation has required historians to re-examine the basis for the more important Cold War decisions and the framework within which administration policy-makers operated.

Until recently, the standard interpretation of the Cold War depicted containment as a belated but necessary response to Soviet intransigence and expansionism. This view has been sustained in the annual studies published by the Council on Foreign Relations, particularly the series edited by John C. Campbell (for the years 1945–1949) and Richard P. Stebbins (for the years 1949–1953). William H. McNeill, *America, Britain and Russia: Their Cooperation and Conflict* (London: Oxford University Press, 1953) remains the best account of the wartime diplomacy of the Big Three. In *Memoirs, 1925–1950* (Boston: Little, Brown, 1967), George F. Kennan, the father of "containment," indirectly outlines his own assumptions and objectives as well as those of State Department policy-makers. *Speaking Frankly* (New York: Harper, 1947) and *All in One Lifetime* (New York: Harper & Row, 1958), the personal accounts of Truman's first Secretary of State, James F. Byrnes, though distinctly partisan, constitute a valuable source of information about administration methods and priorities.

Invaluable, because of his privileged access to State Department papers and those of key policy-makers which have only recently been declassified, are the many volumes of Herbert Feis. Feis's books have provided an indirect research source for other less privileged historians, though his failure to footnote specific documents has reduced the value of his work. These omissions have made it difficult to distinguish between Feis's opinions and documentary evidence. Among the subjects discussed by Feis are: Far Eastern policy, *The China Tangle* (New York: Atheneum paperback, 1965); summit diplomacy and the early postwar years, *Between War and Peace* (Princeton: Princeton University Press, 1960) and *Churchill, Roosevelt, Stalin* (Princeton, Princeton University Press, 1957); wartime policy objectives and the decision to drop the bomb, *Japan Subdued* (Princeton: Princeton University Press, 1961); and postwar occupation in Japan, *Contest over Japan* (New York: Norton, 1967).

Decision in Germany is a revealing, anti-Soviet account by the former deputy military governor general and later military governor of the U.S. zone in Germany, Lucius Clay, which seeks to explain and justify policy toward occupied Germany during the immediate postwar years. An equally anti-Soviet study, of questionable scholarship, is John R. Deane, *The Strange Alliance* (New York, Viking Press, 1947), a revealing source on the dominant assumptions of U.S. policy-makers. Deane was head of the American military mission to Moscow during World War II. William Leahy, a military adviser to Roosevelt at the various wartime conferences and a close, important adviser to Truman after the war, has written a study of administration policy concentrating on summit diplomacy, *I Was There* (New York: Whittlesey House, 1950). Written in the same vein, though focusing on the postwar years, is Walter Bedell Smith, *My Three Years in Moscow* (Philadelphia: Lippincott, 1950). Smith was head of the U.S. mission to Moscow during 1946–

1949 and subsequently director of the CIA. *The Forrestal Diaries* (New York: Viking Press, 1951), edited by Walter Millis, remains an excellent source on the thinking of Truman's Secretary of the Navy and then Secretary of Defense and other key administration advisers whose comments on contemporary crises and decisions are infrequently quoted in this diary. An important volume, if far less valuable then Forrestal's because of the absence of documents on key foreign and domestic policy matters, is *The Private Papers of Senator Vandenberg* (Boston: Houghton Mifflin, 1952), edited by the Senator's son, Arthur Vandenberg, Jr. The U.S. Ambassador to China during 1946–1949, John Leighton Stuart, has analyzed U.S. China policy, and particularly postwar differences with the Chinese Nationalists, in *Fifty Years in China* (New York: Random House, 1954).

The volumes published by the Department of State, though admittedly edited, are an essential source of information. Containing the policy briefs and correspondence of State Department personnel, these volumes cover a variety of subjects. *The Foreign Relations of the United States: The Conference at Malta and Yalta 1945* (Washington: U.S. Government Printing Office, 1955) and *Foreign Relations: Conference of Berlin (Potsdam) 1945* (Washington: U.S. Government Printing Office, 1960) contain the working papers of these important wartime conferences. *Making the Peace Treaties, 1941–1947* (Washington: U.S. Government Printing Office, 1947) includes the texts of the armistice agreements and formal peace treaties, and documents which outline U.S.-Soviet differences and reveal the basis for U.S. concerns in postwar Eastern Europe; and *United States Relations with China* (Washington: U.S. Government Printing Office, 1949) includes the famous White Paper issued in 1949 to defend U.S. policy and to explain the Communists' military success.

The dominant interpretation of the Cold War, which reflects the shift in American diplomatic historiography to emphasize power and strategic considerations in contrast to earlier more romantic and simplistic rationalizations of U.S. diplomacy, is offered by the "realist" school. The themes of this school are (1) the need to advance the national interest through reliance on power arrangements and (2) the acceptance of limitations on U.S. power and influence. The most important exponent of this position is Hans J. Morgenthau of the University of Chicago.

His seminal *In Defense of the National Interest* (New York: Alfred A. Knopf, 1951) states the main realist arguments and has strongly influenced the tactical responses of administration policy-makers. Refining these points and applying them specifically to the European theater, Robert E. Osgood's *Limited War: The Challenge to American Strategy* (Chicago: University of Chicago Press, 1957) offers a sophisticated rationale for a diplomacy based on the flexible use of power. William Reitzel, *et al., United States Foreign Policy 1945–1955* (Washington: Brookings Institution, 1956) is at best a sketchy summary of the period; its value lies in the authors' rationalization of U.S. diplomacy during the decade. Tang Tsou's *America's Failure in China, 1941–1950* (Chicago: University of Chicago Press, 1963) remains by far the best summary of postwar administration China policy. Based on extensive primary research, the book is most critical of the administration's failure to exercise sufficient American influence and power.

The publications of the Rand Corporation, the Air Force's "think tank," constitute another source for realist thinking outside the administration. Representative of this emphasis on the importance of military power are Paul Hammond, "The NSC [National Security Council] as a Device for Interdepartment Co-ordination," *American Political Science Review,* LIV (December 1960), 899–910, and "NSC 68: Prologue to Rearmament," in Warner Schilling, *et al., Strategy, Politics, and Defense Budgets* (New York: Columbia University Press, 1962). These essays document, from a sympathetic perspective, the increasing influence of the military on U.S. policy, specifically the National Security Council's role in shaping American defense spending and coordinating relations between the Defense and State Departments. A less sophisticated, more anti-Soviet study extolling military containment is Bernard Brodie's *The Communist Reach for Empire* (Santa Monica: Rand, P–2916, 1964).

Some works not identified with the realist school are nevertheless invaluable sources on administration diplomacy leading to containment: John Gimbel, *The American Occupation of Germany* (Stanford: Stanford University Press, 1968); Joseph Jones, *The Fifteen Weeks* (New York: Viking Press, 1955), an inside account of the process by which the Truman Doctrine and Marshall Plan were formulated and popularly expounded; and Harry B. Price, *The Marshall Plan and Its Meaning* (Ithaca:

Cornell University Press, 1955), an analytical defense of the Marshall Plan based on access to government records and interviews with key administration personnel. Coral Bell, *Negotiations from Strength* (New York: Alfred A. Knopf, 1963) traces the qualitative shift in U.S. policy during the 1950's from a defensive to a rigid posture based on superior military strength. An invaluable study, embracing the development of the wartime atomic program, the subsequent establishment of the Atomic Energy Commission, and U.S. diplomacy during the war and immediate postwar years, is Richard Hewlett and Oscar Anderson, *The New World, 1939–1946* (University Park, Pa.: Pennsylvania State University Press, 1962).

Revisionist historians, in contrast, have questioned the basic assumptions of containment. Either by emphasizing mutual U.S.-Soviet responsibility or by tracing the origins of the Cold War to American economic expansionism, they have brought about a reappraisal of Cold War politics. Their emphases, whether on mutual or American responsibility, disclose the interpretive differences that also exist within this "school." Sharing a common critical view of postwar administration diplomacy and questioning the self-righteousness of administration policy rhetoric and the analyses of most traditional historians, the revisionists' divergence derives from the weight they give to economic factors or to policy considerations in the making of postwar foreign policy. Fundamentally this divergence rests on the question of whether the Truman administration directly or indirectly repudiated Roosevelt's policy objectives and whether Roosevelt's diplomacy actually provided the basis for the widening postwar rift.

The most influential of the economic "expansionists" is William Appleman Williams. In *The Tragedy of American Diplomacy* (New York: Dell paperback, 1961) and more recently in *The Roots of the Modern American Empire* (New York: Random House, 1970), Williams argues that American foreign policy, expansionist since the 1890's, contributed to the post-war conflict with the Soviet Union by an essentially imperialistic diplomacy. These same themes, though with different emphases on aspects of American diplomacy or policy-makers, are contained in the writings of Gabriel Kolko, *The Politics of War* (New York: Random House, 1968), a study of Roosevelt's wartime diplomacy; Lloyd C. Gardner, *Architects of Illusion*

(Chicago: Quadrangle Books, 1970), a study of key Roosevelt-Truman administration policy advisers; and Walter LaFeber, *America, Russia and the Cold War, 1945–1966* (New York: John Wiley, 1967), an analysis of the origins and militarization of postwar U.S. diplomacy, which stresses the importance of particular American economic objectives and the obsession with power of administration policy-makers. In *Politics and Policies of the Truman Administration,* edited by Barton J. Bernstein (Chicago: Quadrangle Books, 1970), several essayists have examined the assumptions underlying the Marshall Plan (Thomas G. Paterson), the origins of the Cold War (Barton J. Bernstein), and U.S. policy toward Germany (Lloyd C. Gardner) and Latin America (David Green).

In contrast to this economic emphasis, other revisionist historians have stressed either the shift in U.S. diplomacy following Truman's accession to the presidency, or a growing belief in American omnipotence among policy-makers. Gar Alperovitz, *Atomic Diplomacy: Hiroshima and Potsdam* (New York: Simon and Schuster, 1965) concludes that the U.S. atomic monopoly encouraged Truman to adopt a less conciliatory stance toward the Soviet Union and to oppose Soviet influence in Eastern Europe. D. F. Fleming, *The Cold War and Its Origins, 1917–1960,* 2 vols. (Garden City, N.Y.: Doubleday, 1961) has placed the Cold War in a historical context, tracing postwar tensions to suspicions between the United States and the Soviet Union since the 1917 Bolshevik Revolution and stressing the mutual responsibility for the breakdown of the wartime alliance. Martin Herz, a Foreign Service officer, in *Beginnings of the Cold War* (Bloomington: University of Indiana Press, 1966) has dispassionately reviewed U.S. objectives in 1945, noting the concessions made by Roosevelt in 1944 and 1945. His short book effectively discounts the oversimplified view that the Soviet Union unilaterally abrogated the Yalta agreements, and indirectly documents the Truman administration's basic shift away from wartime efforts at collaboration and concession.

Loyalty-Security

Part of the distinctiveness of the Truman administration, besides its contribution to the militarization of American foreign policy, rests on its creation of a permanent, centralized internal-security program. The major changes wrought by Truman include the greater independence, appropriations, and stature of the FBI; the institution of a federal employee loyalty program wary of individual beliefs and associations; the legitimation of loyalty checks and the stigmatizing of certain organizations as "subversive"; and the administration's educational role in helping to enact internal-security legislation which circumscribed traditionally protected liberties. While revolutionary in their implications for national politics and values, these developments have not commanded much attention among historians. (But within the legal profession the major legislative changes, the nature and procedures of the loyalty program, and the major decisions of the Vinson Court have been intensively examined in the law journals.) This dereliction or relative inattention is the result of the more dramatic importance of foreign policy decisions, the restrictions on access to primary sources imposed by the Department of Justice and the FBI, the byproduct of Truman's March 1948 Executive Order imposing secrecy on loyalty reports, and the historian's fascination with the other side of the coin—McCarthyite repression.

Yet a decent body of literature exists, discussing separately Truman's loyalty program, the FBI, the House Committee on Un-American Activities, and the major postwar loyalty cases. Significantly, these studies have touched on particular loyalty-security decisions or events, but none provides an overall appraisal of the loyalty-security question in the Cold War period or attempts to appraise the relationship between the adoption of loyalty procedures and fundamental changes in national politics.

Robert K. Carr, *The House Committee on Un-American Activities, 1945–1950* (Ithaca: Cornell University Press, 1952) has written a solid, critical study of the immediate postwar history of HUAC, concentrating on the committee's unfairness and publicity-seeking. Walter Goodman, *The Committee* (New York: Farrar, Straus and Giroux, 1968), although broader in scope of inquiry and chronology, is far less critical of HUAC and more willing to accept the seriousness of the security threat during the 1930's and 1940's. Written in the same vein as Goodman's book, Earl Latham, *The Communist Controversy in Washington* (Cambridge, Mass., Harvard University Press, 1966) concedes the existence of a serious communist threat, accepts uncritically the findings of congressional committees, and attributes the emergence of McCarthyism to an unbalance between the executive and legislative branches that developed under Roosevelt and Truman. Latham's study is representative of the major themes of Cold War liberalism: a pronounced anti-communism and a tendency to focus on extremes and abuses rather than on the loyalty question *per se*. Similarly, Herbert Packer, *Ex-Communist Witnesses* (Stanford: Stanford University Press, 1962) analyzes the testimony of four communist informers (Whittaker Chambers, Elizabeth Bentley, Louis Budenz, and John Lautner) and their contribution to the development of the loyalty-security obsession. Conceding the need for improved internal-security safeguards, Packer nonetheless criticizes the unfairness and partisanship of postwar congressional investigations and concludes that fairer, more efficient fact-finding processes are needed in matters of internal security.

The Alger Hiss case, the most significant and symbolic of the postwar loyalty cases, has been the subject of innumerable books and articles. Despite the extensive, and often emotional, coverage, the issues involved in the case and particularly the question of Hiss's guilt or innocence remain unresolved. In many respects there is a striking parallel between the Hiss case and the Sacco-Vanzetti case of the 1920's. Whittaker Chambers, in *Witness* (New York: Random House, 1952) and *Cold Friday* (New York: Random House, 1964), defends his own role in the case, seeks to rationalize the inconsistencies and contradictions of his testimony before HUAC, the federal grand jury, and in the course of the 1949 trials, and offers an apocalyptic interpretation of Western civilization current among conservative intellectuals. Alger Hiss's *In the Court of Public Opinion* (New York: Alfred A. Knopf, 1957) is essentially a lawyer's defense brief. In a thorough exposition of the issues of the case, Hiss emphasizes Chambers' duplicity, and, attempting to explain the evidence, develops the thesis of "forgery by typewriter." Alistair Cooke, *A Generation on Trial* (New York: Alfred A. Knopf, 1952) and Earl Jowitt, *The Strange Case of Alger Hiss* (Garden City, N.Y.: Doubleday, 1953) are sympathetic to Hiss. They raise important questions about American society, and relate the case to the climate of opinion in the 1930's and in the postwar period. Meyer Zeligs, a practicing psychiatrist, in *Friendship and Fratricide* (New York: Viking Press, 1967), presents a psychological interpretation of the Hiss-Chambers relationship, including in-depth interviews with Hiss (though not Chambers) and perceptive insights into the writings of both men. However intriguing in its dissection of personalities, Zelig's book adds little to an understanding of the specific issues and thus the controversy still shrouding the case.

Presenting opposite conclusions, Ralph DeToledano and Victor Lasky, *Seeds of Treason* (New York: Funk and Wagnalls, 1950) and DeToledano's "The Alger Hiss Story," *American Mercury* (June 1953), emphasize Hiss's guilt and confirm the existence of a serious internal-security threat. Richard M. Nixon in *Six Crises* (Garden City, N.Y., Doubleday, 1962) discusses his role in the development of the case, while reaffirming Hiss's guilt and the laxity of Democratic security procedures.

The Hiss case has led indirectly to a consideration of the role of the House Committee on Un-American Activities during the Cold War period as well as a judgment about the priorities and actions of the FBI. Necessarily, the issue of loyalty-security in the Cold War involves the increasing postwar power and influence of the FBI. Fred Cook, a free-lance writer and frequent contributor to *The Nation*, has written a debunking critique, *The FBI Nobody Knows* (New York: Pyramid paperback, 1964). In direct contrast, Don Whitehead, *The FBI Story* (New York: Random House, 1956), based on personal interviews and privileged access to FBI sources, uncritically defends the FBI and Hoover against their liberal and radical detractors. The Whitehead study is valuable as a source of information about the major events of the period and about the Bureau's priorities. In a defense of Julius and Ethel Rosenberg, Walter and Miriam Schneir, *Invitation to an Inquest* (Garden City, N.Y.: Doubleday, 1965) raise many probing questions about their conviction for espionage, are critical of the deficiencies of the defense lawyers, document the zealous commitment of the Department of Justice to secure conviction, and suggest that the Department by unfair and questionable procedures (including the forging of a hotel register by the FBI) created a repressive atmosphere that made conviction possible. For an interesting critique of the Schneirs' position, see Allen Weinstein's article "Agit-Prop & the Rosenbergs," in *Commentary*, July 1970, pp. 18–25.

By far the most important development in the postwar internal-security scare, Truman's institution of a federal loyalty program in 1947, is discussed in depth by a number of prominent political scientists and legal scholars. Still the best survey of the loyalty program, though written in the early 1950's, is Eleanor Bontecou's *The Federal Loyalty-Security Program* (Ithaca: Cornell University Press, 1953), a sometimes critical study of the loyalty procedures instituted under Truman. Conceding the need for effective loyalty procedures beyond those traditionally relied on by the federal government, Miss Bontecou is primarily critical of certain excesses. Similar criticisms of loyalty procedures, consistent with this attempt to balance considerations of internal security and individual liberties, are detailed in Harold Chase, *Security and Liberty: The Problem of Native Communists* (Garden City, N.Y.: Doubleday, 1955) and Ralph S. Brown, Jr., *Loyalty and Security* (New Haven: Yale University Press, 1958). *Political and Civil Rights in the United States,* Vol. I (Boston: Little, Brown, 1967), by Thomas Emerson, David Haber, and Norman Dorsen, contains an excellent discussion of national security, the loyalty program, and political freedoms. This book, a law student case study, includes excerpts from the major court cases, executive orders, and legislation. It also provides commentary and an extensive bibliography on the constitutional and libertarian issues raised by these postwar developments. Francis Biddle, *In Brief Authority* (New York: Doubleday, 1962); Alan Barth, *The Loyalty of Free Men* (New York: Viking Press, 1951); and Thomas Emerson and David Helfeld, "Loyalty Among Government Employees," *Yale Law Journal,* LVIII (December 1948), 1–143, question the necessity and discuss the repressive ramifications of the loyalty procedures instituted by the Truman administration and Congress. C. Herman Pritchett, *Civil Liberties and the Vinson Court* (Chicago: University of Chicago Press, 1954), a critical account of the Supreme Court during Truman's presidency, discusses the major constitutional and libertarian issues raised by the Court's decisions, particularly in the *Dennis* and *Doud* cases.

McCarthyism

The McCarthy phenomenon, extensively and often emotionally analyzed, has dominated postwar writings in much the same way as earlier it dominated national politics. Books and articles about McCarthyism, both popular and academic, have been decidedly subjective, whether because of the lack of intensive research into the available primary sources or the emotions that the movement elicited. These analyses have not been confined to Mc-Carthyism as a distinct political movement; they are essentially impressionistic studies of American society and mass politics and lead directly to judgments about the American character, the nature of American politics, the desirability of consensus, and ultimately the significance and ramifications of McCarthy's impact during the 1950's. Essential to any preliminary understanding is a recently published, extremely useful summary of the McCarthy phenomenon edited by Allen J. Matusow, *Joseph R. McCarthy* (Englewood Cliffs, N.J.: Prentice-Hall, 1970). This book contains representative selections from McCarthy's speeches and from the literature on McCarthyism, and the editor has provided useful introductory comments and a thorough, annotated bibliography. Supplementing this is the Senator's own disappointing study, *McCarthyism: The Fight for America* (New York: Devin-Adair, 1952). McCarthy's book disappoints because it contains no more information than is already available to the reader of the popular press or the *Congressional Record*. The book is really only a recapitulation of the themes that McCarthy raised in Congress or in public speeches. William F. Buckley and L. Brent Bozell, in *McCarthy and His Enemies* (Chicago: Regnery, 1954), offer a more sophisticated defense of McCarthyism. Conceding that McCarthy might have exaggerated his charges, and that they were sometimes undocumented if not wrong, the authors nonetheless commend the Senator for forcing public consideration and understanding of the communist issue. Buckley and Bozell emphasize the seriousness of the security threat, which administration leaders sought to ignore, and use the McCarthy phenomenon to impugn the loyalty and priorities of McCarthy's liberal and radical critics. Their study is perhaps most revealing of the main themes and priorities of American conservatives in the postwar period, particularly their conceptions of individual liberties, reform, and international policy. A more intemperate defense of McCarthy is William Schlamm's obituary, "Across McCarthy's Grave," *National Review*, III (May 18, 1957), 469–470. Representing McCarthy as a victim of malice, martyred because of his principled convictions and integrity, Schlamm puts the blame on liberalism and relativism.

The critical literature on McCarthy is equally partisan and intemperate. Richard Rovere's *Senator Joe McCarthy* (Cleveland: World, 1960), a well-written and bitterly condemnatory study, stresses the Senator's opportunism and cynicism. Seeking to explain the Senator's impact despite an amazing lack of substance in his accusations, Rovere concentrates on McCarthy's shrewdness in using statistics and seemingly authentic documentation to capture public support. Michael Straight, *Trial by Television* (Boston: Beacon Press, 1954) is a detailed discussion of the Army-McCarthy hearings of 1954. Seeking to explicate the basis for the Senator's influence, Straight raises the themes developed in T. W. Adorno's 1950 study of *The Authoritarian Personality*. James Wechsler, *The Age of Suspicion* (New York: Random House, 1953) adopts a different perspective. Wechsler emphasizes the climate of opinion during the 1930's, discusses his own flirtation with radicalism, and describes how such an experience made many American liberals vulnerable to loyalty charges in the 1950's. *McCarthy, the Man, the Senator, the Ism* (Boston: Beacon Press, 1952), by Jack Anderson and Ronald May, is a hostile, sometimes unfair analysis of the McCarthy phenomenon. As with most liberal critiques of McCarthyism, this book, and more notably that of James Rorty and Moshe Decter, *McCarthy and the Communists* (Boston: Beacon Press, 1954), is most revealing about the priorities and changing values of American liberals. Thus Rorty and Decter, though harshly critical of McCarthy's purposes and methods, seek to establish their own vigilant anti-communism by admitting the seriousness of the internal-security threat and the need for an effective loyalty-security program, and by criticizing McCarthy for aiding the communists. This emotional, often excessive anti-communism is extended in Leslie Fiedler's "McCarthy," *Encounter*, III (August 1954), 10–21. In this article, Fiedler specifically attributes the rise of McCarthy to the liberals' failure to appreciate, and thereby confront, communism's serious threat to the national security. Fiedler's criticisms of McCarthy, like those of Leroy Gore in *Joe Must Go* (New York: Julian Messner, 1954), are confined to the Senator's methods and purposes.

Even the more academic, presumably less partisan, studies of the Senator's impact are concerned with it as a phenomenon of mass irrationality. They fail to consider the timing and substance of the movement. Samuel Lubell, in *The Future of American Politics* (Garden City, N.Y.: Doubleday, 1956), thus explains McCarthyism as a product of Midwestern or ethnic (German, Irish) isolationism, and implicitly questions the viability of democratic politics in the conduct of foreign policy. Representing McCarthy's appeal as primarily to a public overwhelmed by the complex responsibilities of international involvement, Lubell accepts the rationality of administration policy and the expertise of administration policy-makers. Norman Graebner's *The New Isolationism* (New York: Ronald Press, 1956), though not a study of McCarthyism *per se,* stresses the partisanship and irresponsibility of the conservative congressional critique of containment and other administration foreign-policy decisions during the 1950's, thereby making essentially the same judgment as Lubell about the democratic process and the expertise of administration policy-makers. Leo Huberman and Paul Sweezy in "The Roots and Prospects of McCarthyism," *Monthly Review,* V (January 1954), 419–425, offer a simplified Marxian interpretation of McCarthyism: since McCarthy's support came from conservative businessmen—the new rich, Texas oil men, and other parvenus—there is a parallel between McCarthy and Hitler. The authors' representation of McCarthyism as incipient fascism is as deficient as the elitist interpretations of the liberals, because they ignore both the political context and the noneconomic basis for the Senator's popular support. In a limited study based on interviews with the leaders of the corporate business community, Charles J. V. Murphy in "McCarthy and the Businessmen," *Fortune,* XLIX (April 1954), 156–158, 180–194, and "Texas Business and McCarthy," *Fortune,* XLIX (May 1954), 100–101, 208–216, indirectly refutes the Huberman-Sweezy conclusions. Murphy confirms the divergent response to McCarthy among businessmen and identifies his strongest supporters as responding primarily to his attack on presidential power (reflecting their conservative anti-New Dealism), not to the issue of national security. Murphy's study, which ignores the popular base of McCarthy's support, his appeal to small businessmen, and the timing of business criticism of McCarthy, has limited scholarly value. In an impressionistic and suggestive study, based upon limited research, John Steinke and James Weinstein, in "McCarthy and the Liberals," *Studies on the Left,* II (1962) 43–50, argue that liberals created the climate leading to McCarthyism. Steinke and Weinstein specifically emphasize the liberals' responsibility for Cold War policies, and focus narrowly on the 1946 senatorial campaign in Wisconsin.

Distinct from an appraisal of the movement itself (though a direct byproduct), McCarthyism profoundly affected the concepts many American intellectuals have about their society and about past and contemporary political movements. Among historians, McCarthyism has indirectly contributed to the growth of the consensus interpretation of the American past. Taking off from Daniel J. Boorstin's celebration of the pragmatic character of American politics, outlined in his *The Genius of American Politics* (Chicago: University of Chicago Press, 1953), historians of the 1950's and 1960's have explored the uniqueness and greatness of the American experience, attributing its success primarily to the absence of conflict inherent in nonideological politics. This view of American history and its focus on accommodation has coincided with the emergence of more sophisticated historical methods, including interdisciplinary approaches which rely on psychological data. Thus past conflict and dissent have come increasingly to be interpreted in social rather than economic terms.

An index of this change in the interpretation of the American past is conveyed in the writings of Richard Hofstadter. A former radical critic of the failures of American reform politics, the main themes of which are outlined in *The American Political Tradition* (New York: Alfred A. Knopf, 1948), Hofstadter during the 1950's changed his conclusions and came to celebrate consensus politics and criticize earlier reform movements less for the inadequacy of their leadership than for their popular reactionary character. Hofstadter then argued that movements such as populism and progressivism were more emotional than responsive, reactionary rather than presentist, motivated by "status" rather than economic considerations, and that they failed because of their mass, emotional character, not the essential conservatism of their leaders. These themes were first suggested in *The Age of Reform* (New York: Alfred A. Knopf, 1955) and later developed in *The Paranoid Style in American Politics and Other Essays* (New York: Alfred A. Knopf, 1965).

Hofstadter's analysis can be understood not only as a corrective reappraisal of earlier romantic interpretations of populism and progressivism, but as a product of the McCarthy phenomenon which forced leading American intellectuals to reappraise the nature of mass reform movements. Thus other social scientists, whose main themes are contained in *The Radical Right*, edited by Daniel Bell (Garden City, N.Y.: Doubleday, 1964), have begun a critical reappraisal of disruptive, populistic movements. The Bell volume, its contributors the more influential social scientists of the 1950's—Daniel Bell, Richard Hofstadter, David Riesman, Nathan Glazer, Peter Viereck, Talcott Parsons, Alan Westin, Seymour Lipset, Herbert Hyman—implicitly criticizes populistic politics and extols a politics of accommodation. These men have located the motivation for McCarthy not in economic but in social concerns, and have stressed the emotional, nonexpert side of democratic politics. According to this view, during periods of disruptive change the emotional American public, nostalgic about a lost past and overwhelmed by complex, modern problems, has responded to demagogic appeals which offered simplistic, conspiratorial explanations for contemporary crises or problems. In their analysis of McCarthyism, these social scientists have stressed its psychological and not its conservative character, and have represented it as symbolizing the harmfulness of ideological mass politics. These same themes have been elaborated in Daniel Bell, *The End of Ideology* (Glencoe, Ill.: Free Press, 1960); Edward Shils, *The Torment of Secrecy* (Glencoe, Ill.: Free Press, 1956); Nathan Glazer, "The Method of Senator McCarthy," *Commentary*, XV (March 1953), 244–256; Victor Ferkiss, "Political and Intellectual Origins of American Radicalism, Right and Left," *Annals of the American Academy of Political and Social Science*, CCCXLIV (November 1962), 1–12; and Irwin W. Goffman, "Status Consistency and Preference for Change in Power Distribution," *American Sociological Review*, XXII (June 1957), 275–281.

Sharply dissenting from these "status" theoreticians, challenging both their methodology and research, are a series of studies of McCarthyism and past reform movements written primarily by political scientists. *The Intellectuals and McCarthy: The Radical Specter* (Cambridge, Mass.: M.I.T. Press, 1967) by Michael Rogin, an examination of the Hofstadter thesis, brilliantly summarizes the major critique of these younger scholars. Rogin analyzes the sources of Midwestern populism, progressivism, and McCarthyism through an analysis of voting returns, documents the divergent appeal of these movements, and specifically identifies McCarthyism as a form of conservative Republican politics. Emphasizing issues not personality, economic not social or psychological questions, Rogin's study is more a critique of the essential conservatism of the consensus historians than an analysis of the origins of McCarthyism. Rogin suggests that the emotional trauma of their response to McCarthyism led these intellectuals to view all mass efforts at political change as threats to stability, all threats to stability as threats to constitutional democracy. American liberals, he concludes, ventured unwittingly into conservative political theory.

Rogin's study has summarized the conclusions of an impressive body of literature on the McCarthy movement. These sources, in contrast to the approach of Bell *et al.*, have concentrated on McCarthyism as a political movement and have emphasized its conservative impact and purposes. The most important of these studies are Dennis Wrong, "Theories of McCarthyism: A Survey," *Dissent,* I (Autumn 1954), 385–397; David A. Shannon, "Was McCarthy a Political Heir of LaFollette?," *Wisconsin Magazine of History,* XLV (Autumn 1961), 3–9; Nelson W. Polsby, "Towards an Explanation of McCarthyism," *Political Studies,* VIII (October 1960), 250–271; Martin Trow, "Small Businessmen, Political Intolerance, and Support for McCarthy," *American Journal of Sociology,* LXIV (November 1958), 270–281; and Philip Chapman, "The New Conservatism: Cultural Criticism vs. Political Philosophy," *Political Science Quarterly,* LXXV (March 1960), 17–34.

Truman Administration

In view of the major changes during his presidency in the areas of civil liberties, civil rights, foreign policy, and the institutionalization of the office of the presidency, it is surprising that the Truman administration has not received extensive analysis either by historians or journalists. For the most part, writings on the Truman years have focused on specific problems or questions. With the exception of Cabell Phillips' journalistic account, *The Truman Presidency* (New York: MacMillan, 1966), there is no overall appraisal of the administration. In part this is due to the relative closeness of events of the Truman years (historians feel more comfortable with a longer perspective), and in part because of the greater glamor and controversy that attracts historians to the study of the Roosevelt administration, and the extent to which Truman's seems to be a less bold continuation of that presidency. Future historians and political scientists will assuredly correct this neglect. The absence of such studies, however, has contributed to a generally sympathetic view of Truman as a "great" or "near great" President; it has also hampered an intensive examination of the sources of contemporary economic, international, racial, and urban problems.

Most studies of the Truman administration, typical of which are Elmer Cornwell's *Presidential Leadership of Public Opinion* (Bloomington: Indiana University Press, 1965), Eric Goldman's *The Crucial Decade and After: America, 1945–1960* (New York: Vintage paperback, 1960), and Walter Johnson's *1600 Pennsylvania Avenue* (Boston: Little, Brown, 1960), have focused on the institution of the presidency rather than on the tenure of Harry S. Truman. Somewhat critical, these books concur on the need for a strong executive and praise or blame Truman for exercising (or not) the necessary leadership to direct the nation. Liberal in their defense of New Deal–Fair Deal domestic and international policies, these historians have tended to identify liberalism with the national interest and to accept presidential rhetoric and purpose at face value.

In a distinctly different vein, a more skeptical critique of American liberalism and the Truman administration is emerging among younger historians. Working with available primary sources, these historians have not only examined the nature of administration policy and Truman's commitment to reform but have questioned the wisdom and necessity of administration policy. Foremost among these historians is Barton J. Bernstein. In an impressive number of essays, he has challenged many key assumptions about "corporate liberalism" and Truman's domestic and international leadership. The major themes developed by Bernstein are contained in "America in War and Peace: The Test of Liberalism," in *Towards a New Past*, pp. 289–321, edited by Barton J. Bernstein (New York: Pantheon, 1968) and in another essay collection that he edited, *Politics and Policies of the Truman Administration* (Chicago: Quadrangle Books, 1970).

A useful summary of the key decisions and controversies of the Truman years is *The Truman Administration: A Documentary History* (New York: Harper & Row, 1966), edited by Bernstein and Allen J. Matusow. *The Truman Period as a Research Field*, edited by Richard S. Kirkendall (Columbia, Mo.:

University of Missouri Press, 1967), contains an extensive bibliography, a listing of the holdings of the Truman Library, and
a series of essays suggesting research problems in the areas of
military and foreign policy (David McLellan and John Reuss),
economic policy (Barton J. Bernstein), civil rights and civil
liberties (William Berman), social welfare policy (Richard O.
Davies), and the Truman presidency (Elmer Cornwell).

For the most part, scholarly writing on the Truman years
has been topical. The major themes have included the 1948
presidential campaign—R. Alton Lee's "The Turnip Session of
the Do-Nothing Congress: Presidential Campaign Strategy,"
Southwestern Social Science Quarterly (December 1963), a
thorough study of Truman's strategy in winning re-election in
1948; Jules Abels' more conservative analysis of that campaign,
Out of the Jaws of Victory (New York: Holt, 1959), and Karl
Schmidt's sympathetic study of Wallace's Progressive party
campaign, *Henry A. Wallace: Quixotic Campaign 1948* (Syracuse: Syracuse University Press, 1960). Also Truman's agricul-
tural policies—Allen J. Matusow's critical, well-written and
well-researched *Farm Policies and Politics in the Truman Years*
(Cambridge, Mass.: Harvard University Press, 1967); labor
policies and Congress—R. Alton Lee's disappointing *Truman
and Taft-Hartley: A Question of Mandate* (Lexington, Ky.:
University of Kentucky Press, 1966); and Truman's social welfare policies and difficulties with Congress—Richard O. Davies'
brief, sympathetic study of the process which led to the enactment of one of Truman's few legislative achievements, the National Housing Act of 1949, *Housing Reform During the
Truman Administration* (Columbia, Mo.: University of Missouri Press, 1966); and civil rights—Richard Dalfiume's study
of the desegregation of the army, *Desegregation of the U.S.
Armed Forces: Fighting on Two Fronts, 1939–1953* (Columbia,
Mo.: University of Missouri Press, 1969).

The Truman administration has only recently become a major
area of historical study, and historians have so far only skimmed
the primary sources of Truman's congressional and presidential
career. Richard S. Kirkendall and Barton J. Bernstein are now
completing biographies of Truman. A number of other young
scholars, including Alonzo Hamby, Richard Dalfiume, Richard
Davies, Franklin Mitchell, Robert Zangrando, Harvard Sitkoff,

Allen Matusow, William Berman, Thomas Paterson, and Lester Adler, have manuscripts in press or partially completed. When published, their studies will increase our knowledge of this formative presidency, the origins of Cold War anti-communism, the postwar resurgence of conservatism, the structure and responsiveness of Congress and American political institutions, and the relevance of American liberalism for contemporary society.

Index

A Note on the Author

Athan Theoharis was born and grew up in Milwaukee, Wisconsin, and studied at the University of Chicago, where he received a Ph.D. in 1965. His other writings include *The Yalta Myths: An Issue in U.S. Politics, 1945–1955;* essays in two original collections—*Politics and Policies of the Truman Administration* (edited by Barton J. Bernstein) and *Cold War Critics* (edited by Thomas G. Paterson); and articles in such periodicals as the *Political Science Quarterly* and *New University Thought.* Mr. Theoharis is now Associate Professor of American History at Marquette University.